JOURNEY TO FREEDOM

JOURNEY TO FREEDOM

Victory from Addiction Is Closer than You Think!

Mel Steinmeyer

With Brian Ellingson, Jon Carter & Chase Steinmeyer

COPYRIGHT © 2023 Melvin L. Steinmeyer

JOURNEY TO FREEDOM
Victory from Addiction Is Closer than You Think!

All rights reserved. Brief quotations from this book may be used in presentations, articles, and books. Otherwise, no portion of this book may be reproduced in any form without written permission from the publisher or author, except as permitted by U.S. copyright law.

All Scripture quotations, unless otherwise indicated, are taken from the Holy Bible, New International Version®, NIV®. Copyright © 1973, 1978, 1984, 2011 by Biblica, Inc.™ Used by permission of Zondervan. All rights reserved worldwide.

ISBN: 979-8-218-13489-1

Library of Congress Control Number: 2023900958

Editor: Jeff Plake
Cover Art: Emily Jimenez

To Denise,
my bride, my heart, my love,
my best friend for over three decades
who shows me daily what God's grace looks like

CONTENTS

Foreword by Gary Hays

Freedom. We all search for it. Few of us find it completely. There was once a song called *Looking for Love in All the Wrong Places.* The search for freedom can be like that.

Pastor Mel Steinmeyer's struggles with addiction lasted over thirty-seven years. His journey was a battle that raged between human temptations, guilt, secrecy, and faith. In his struggles, he felt his personal power would be enough to overcome his dark temptations. It wasn't.

Many of us choose to fix ourselves through self-motivation and willpower. Mel discusses how this is often a failing exercise.

Alcoholics talk about "hitting the bottom of the bottle" before they are forced to look up and release themselves to a "higher power." Like Mel, they discover that freedom is often a decision away. Choosing to walk toward Christ is ultimately more powerful than our human efforts of running away from addiction.

Paul encourages us in Romans 12:2, *"Do not conform any longer to the pattern of this world, but be transformed by the renewing of your mind."*

Pastor Mel's story is a story of renewal. It is a story of finding freedom from the chains of addiction by allowing the "Chain Cutter" to do his work. It is a story of a simple yet profound decision to be transformed by the truth and grace of Christ. It is a story of how that decision provided all the power necessary to set him free. Freedom from addiction. Freedom to live the life Jesus intends for all of us.

Freedom is no longer a *choice* for Pastor Mel but a natural response to his relationship in Christ. An exhale to the breathing-in of God.

If you are struggling with temptations or addictions (or if you know someone who is), Pastor Mel's story and teachings can bring you hope. It can bring you encouragement. And it can help you take a closer step toward the One who holds your freedom in his hands.

Rev. Gary Hays
Global Director, thinkSMALL Ministries
www.thinksmallglobal.org

1

"FREEDOM!"

Do we really need another book about how to get free from pornography (or any addiction for that matter)? The simple answer is "yes" ...and "no." I say "yes" because almost every one of the books I have read about addiction (including addiction to porn) is about controlling our addictions and not about true freedom from addiction. On the other hand, I say "no" because there is already a book that has been written that can set you free. It's the Bible...which is not just a book, but the very Word of God. This, in fact, is why it is "alive and active"[1] and is able to do what ordinary books written by mere men cannot do.

Yet many addicts have read the Bible, are true followers of Jesus, and are still not free, though Jesus promised we would be. Is this you? I'll tell you the truth. This was me. I was addicted to pornography for thirty-seven years, and, for all but about four of those years, I was a follower of Jesus. Furthermore, for many of those years, I was a pastor. I knew the Bible. I had read it from cover to cover many times. I believed it (or thought I did). However, I continued to live a secret life as a porn addict.

Sometimes I could control it (and I really wanted to) to some degree by having an accountability partner, by installing a software filter to protect my eyes from even seeing internet porn, by making a "covenant with my eyes" as Job said he did[2] and averting my eyes when I *did* happen to stumble into porn (or at least I tried to), by taking authority over demonic temptation (at least I said the words I was taught to say), and by confessing that I was free (though I sure didn't feel free and knew in my heart that I was going to mess up again). I did everything the books, the preachers, and the so-called experts told me to do. However, true freedom eluded me. Like I said, I knew I was going to blow it eventually…and I did. In fact, for many of the years I struggled with porn, I couldn't make it through a complete month without messing up in some way.

However, I have now been walking in complete freedom for more than six years. I *believe* I'm free, I *know* I'm free, and I *feel* free! This does not mean that I'm now impenetrable and it's impossible for me to slip in some way. However, I don't believe I will, and this is a far cry from the world I lived in and came to accept as truth for me. Oh, by the way, since it's *freedom* I have and not just *control*, it's *easy*. Let me say that again. It's *easy*! I don't have to "battle" (like many of the books direct us to do), and I don't even need an accountability partner (though I still have one).

I love the scene in *Braveheart* where Mel Gibson – portraying William Wallace – with his last breath cries out, "FREEDOM!" This is the truth I'm declaring about me. And this is the invitation I am extending to you. True freedom is possible, and it's *easy*.

Six months into my new freedom, I couldn't keep my mouth shut about it. Six months may not seem like a very long time to some people, but for an addict, it's an eternity. I wanted everyone to know. My heart was completely healed, my shame was gone, and I was free! Furthermore, like I said, it was *easy*. I wanted to help other men to know this freedom for themselves. However, when I shared my story, I couldn't help but notice that faraway look in so many eyes. So many of the men I tried to help just didn't believe me. It was just too good to be true. So, I prayed, "Lord, why don't they believe me?"

Now, I'm one of those "weirdos" that believe God actually wants to speak to his people (his followers, his children), and that his sheep hear his voice.[3] Throughout my life I have heard God speak to me on a regular basis. This time, what I heard the Lord reply to my heart was: "Would you have believed you five years ago?"

Of course, my answer was, "No." Like I said, it was just too good to be true...and way too *easy* to be believed.

"The reason you believe," the Holy Spirit continued speaking to my heart, "is because you've been on a journey so you *could* believe. So, I want you to write a book about your journey to freedom." This is that book. And this is that journey…*my journey to freedom.*

This is not a psychological book. In my journey, I read some books like that, and they helped me to better understand addiction. In addition, they helped me to come to grips with some of my deep wounds that led to my addiction in the first place and which kept me steeped in it, medicating my pain through pornography.

However, Jesus made it very clear that lust is sin. In fact, he declared that when we lust, we are committing adultery in our hearts.[4] Pornography is all about lust and coveting. Its very design is to provide something for and in your mind that is not yours and does not belong to you. It is wrong and, in fact, sin. Of course, I probably don't need to tell you that. You already know this in your heart. And though there might be psychological reasons why we turn to pornography (or any addiction for that matter), at its core it is a spiritual problem in need of a spiritual solution. In other words, psychology may help us better *understand* why we are broken, but only Jesus can heal us from sin. With that said, this book is my account of my *spiritual* journey to freedom.

In fact, I would even contend that I didn't really even need to understand addiction or why I'm broken in order to be healed (although both of these things were part of my own journey to freedom). Think of all the people in the Bible who were completely healed by Jesus long before Freud, Piaget, Skinner, or Jung were even born. It turns out that their remedy was simple: they admitted they were sick, recognized that Jesus was the Healer, *and believed!* Those who were in bondage admitted they were captive, received Jesus as their Deliverer, *and believed!* And those who were sinners humbled themselves before Jesus, the Holy One, *and believed!*

This book is not a bunch of rules or guidelines you to need to follow in order to control your addiction. That is the law, and it is powerless to set you free. My brother-in-law, Jon Carter, when sharing with our church his own journey to freedom, put it this way: "Jesus didn't come to build you a stronger cage; he came to set you free!" There are plenty of books about helping you build a better cage. This book, however, is different. This book is about *believing* and growing that faith. In other words, it is about the Gospel, the Good News, and how after many years of being a Christian and even a pastor, I finally came to understand it for what it was and is. Oh yeah, and I *believed it!*

This book is written for you. I really want to help YOU. Since *realizing* my own freedom (you will come to understand what I mean by that as you follow my journey), I have helped several other men to realize their freedom as well. In fact, at the end of this book, you'll get to hear from a couple of those men. *They* want to help you too.

This is the book I wish someone had written for *me* years ago.

"FREEDOM!"

2

"You're Already Free"

It was the evening before our first Faith Discovery Class. This class was the result of a dream I had. Not a dream like an envisioning, but a literal dream in the middle of the night. In Acts 2:17 it says, *"In the last days...your young men will see visions, your old men will dream dreams."* I guess that makes it official then: I'm old. Anyway, in the dream, I saw myself teaching a class for people who were just starting out on this faith-journey-in-Christ thang as well as for people who were struggling to believe or had "lost their faith," so to speak.

At our church, we had already offered a class called "Grace Discovery." However, now God was giving me a dream for a *new* class about discovering faith. Both classes were based on the S.O.A.P. model for reading the Bible, made famous by Wayne Cordiero.[1] S.O.A.P. stands for

Scripture, Observation, Application, and Prayer. The way we would use this Bible study method in our discovery classes was, instead of just teaching material about grace or faith, we would have the participants read some passages of scripture and write down their own personal observations from what they read. Then we would share with the class what each of us discovered, discuss and figure how we should apply it to our lives, and then pray for one another. In other words, instead of being lectured about grace or faith, the participants would discover grace and faith for themselves. I'll share more about that particular class in chapter eight. However, let's go back to that evening before that class.

As I arrived home from a day at the office, my wife, Denise, informed me that a book I had ordered had arrived. The name of the book was *Feels Like Redemption* by Seth Taylor.[2] For years, I used XXXchurch software (which would send a record of my internet usage to an accountability partner and vice versa). As a result of using this service, I would also receive promotional and encouraging communications from XXXchurch founder Craig Gross. In one of those emails, Craig recommended this book, and for some reason (I'll call it the Holy Spirit's prompting) I felt compelled to order it.

Now it had arrived – and on the eve of this class that I had dreamt about. Again, I sensed an urgency, so I broke it open and dove right in. On the issue of pornography, Seth talked about it in ways I had never heard discussed before.

He shared about his own struggles with lust, how he confessed this to his counselor, and how his counselor gave him a book to read about how lust is *Every Man's Battle.* After reading this book, Seth felt encouraged that he was not alone in his struggle. However, it did not set him free.[3] Years ago, I had read that same book as well as many like it, and these books didn't set *me* free either. On the other hand, just like Seth had experienced, I too felt better knowing I was not the only one struggling with this issue. The old adage is so true: "misery loves company."

One of the things that I appreciated most about Seth's psychological perspective was his contrast between control and true healing. Control is only "*temporary* relief from the symptoms of our pain."[4] Control is about attempting to hold something in and contain it. However, he explains, "Like a vault with too much contained inside, our pain will always find a way out."[5] Often, our pain finds its way out of us through an addiction. True healing, on the other hand, does not just deal with the symptoms of our pain but gets to the heart of the issue, and so it's permanent.

Addiction, by its very definition, is the inability to say "no" to what we are addicted to. This is why trying to control an addiction is so difficult, if not futile. For most of us, rather than controlling our addiction, our addiction is controlling us. However, when true healing takes place and true freedom is experienced, we *can* say "no." And because we're empowered to say "no," freedom *feels* free.

That night, as I poured over the first sixty-something pages of that book, I came face to face with a truth I never realized: I was just controlling my addiction, and that is why it would leak out from time to time. Furthermore, even though I had been a follower of Jesus since I was seventeen, I had never felt free except for the moment of my salvation when I literally felt my sins being lifted from me. However, that was a long time ago, and I had grown to accept that my life was what it was until I died. *Then* I would be with Jesus, and *then* I would *finally* be free. Yet, as I read those pages, and as this idea that *"freedom oughta' feel free"* whirred in my head, a new possibility began to stir in my heart.

My wife knew of my lifelong struggles in this area, and we talked freely about it that night. She loves me unconditionally and knows that my issue was not about her but about a deep wound in my heart. She prays for me and has even "rebuked me" for not being more honest with her when I have been tempted. She wants to know so she can pray for me. Her attitude towards me and "my issue" has been so healing for me. However, I would rather be free than just understood. I would rather be free for her sake and for mine. She deserves a man who walks in complete freedom in this area.

After we talked awhile…it was getting late…I turned over in our bed with my back to her and began to pray. In the first chapter of this book, I mentioned how I actually believe God wants to speak to his children and that he has spoken to me on a regular basis throughout the years. He has never spoken to me audibly but more like whispers to my heart. However, there are a handful of times in my life where his whisper was so clear that it was piercing. This night would be one of those times. This is what I prayed, and this is the question I cried out to God: "Jesus, after all these years, can I finally be free?"

And this is what I heard so clearly in reply: "Mel, you're already free. You just haven't realized it yet."

This book is about my journey to freedom and the steps that led me to *realizing* my freedom. Freedom oughta' feel free! Friend, if you don't *feel* free, then follow me, and I'll show you how to get there. Are you ready? Let's dive in!

3

First Things First

"The definition of insanity is doing the same thing over and over and expecting different results."[1]

"If you do what you've always done, you'll get what you've always got."[2]

Both of the above quotes make perfect sense. Yet many of us stuck in addiction stay stuck because we continue to do the same things over and over again, hoping and praying that *this time* it will finally work. However, if we are going to experience true freedom, we are going to have to change some things.

When John the Baptist preached in the wilderness, preparing hearts for the coming of Jesus, and before he baptized those who responded, he told them that they needed to repent.[3]

When Jesus began to proclaim the Good News (the Gospel) saying that the *"The time has come"* and that *"The kingdom of God has come near,"* he told those listening that they needed to repent (and believe the Good News).[4]

When Jesus sent his disciples out to share this good news, they told the people that they should repent.[5]

On the day the Holy Spirit was poured out on the church, Peter explained to the people how this was the fulfillment of a promise given long ago. And when the people were "cut to the heart" and on the verge of *finally* believing, they asked him, "What should we do?" Peter replied that they should repent (and be baptized in the name of Jesus…).[6]

When the Apostle Paul shared the good news about Jesus everywhere he went, he told everyone he shared with that they should repent (and turn to God…).[7]

Obviously, before anything else, the first thing we need to do is *repent*. However, what does it mean to repent? What does that word even mean? What do you think it means? What were you taught? For many of us, that word might have a negative connotation. Maybe it makes you think of a very serious preacher, sweating profusely, veins popping out of his neck, and screaming at the top of his lungs, *"REPENT OR DIE!"..."TURN OR BURN!"* Is that what repent means?

I ask this of people all the time when I'm trying to help

them follow Jesus. Almost *all* of them say something like this, "To feel sorry for, mourn, or regret your behavior…to change your ways or behavior…you're walking one way, but then you turn around and walk the other way…a 180° change of behavior." Sound familiar? Is that what you were taught? That's what I was taught. In fact, that is what *I taught* for years and years. WE WERE WRONG! Not in that it was wrong to feel sorry for our behavior or to try to change our ways or to teach others to do the same. However, we had *missed the point* of what true biblical repentance is *according to Jesus and the New Testament.* I feel bad about this, but I didn't know any better, just as the person who taught you probably didn't know any better either. After all, that is what we were taught by the people who mentored us. While this may be what the idea of repentance is in the Old Testament, that's not what John the Baptist, Jesus, his disciples, Peter, and the Apostle Paul were saying.

In every case I cited above, the word translated "repent" is from the Greek word *"metanoia"* (or some version of this word). If you look up *metanoia* on Merriam-Webster's online dictionary, it will define this word as "a transformative *change of heart* [italics mine] – especially a spiritual conversion." Merriam-Webster defines this word this way because in our modern world that's the predominant understanding of this word. However, that's not what *metanoia* means…or at least that's not what it *meant* when Jesus and the Apostle Paul were using it. And, in fact, even Merriam-Webster bears this out, saying this about the history and etymology (the study of words, their origin, and the way in which their meanings have changed throughout history) of this word: 'Greek, from *metanoiein* - to change one's mind, repent; from *meta-* + *noein,* to think, from *nous,* mind.'[8]

Good and solid biblical interpretation always seeks to discover the *original* intent and meaning of the author at the time when the words were spoken or written down. Therefore, understanding what "repent" means *now* is a moot point. I want to know what Jesus meant when he spoke this word! And in his days, the word metanoia meant "to change one's mind about someone or something." Whether it was classical Greek literature or Hellenistic Jewish writings of that time period, *metanoia* was used consistently "to express a fundamental change in thinking that leads to a fundamental change in behavior and/or way of living."[9]

When the Bible was first translated into Latin, the word metanoia was translated to *paenitentia* which came to mean "penance" or "acts of penance." However, Tertullian (the well-known Christian apologist and a polemicist against heresy and the first one to use the word "Trinity" to describe the Father, Son, and Holy Spirit) protested this translation, stating that "in Greek, metanoia is not a confession of sins but a change of mind."[10]

Unfortunately, many of the more modern translations of the Bible did not listen to Tertullian and as a result, we continue to propagate the idea that repentance is a changing of our behaviors and hearts rather than a changing of our thinking. As a result, *some of us might have to change our thinking about what repent means. And, by the way, this is vital if we truly want to walk in freedom.*

John the Baptist was not telling people to clean up their lives in a vain effort to somehow make themselves acceptable for the coming Messiah. On the contrary, he was telling them they needed to change their thinking so they *wouldn't miss* the Messiah and so that they might recognize that Jesus was him. When Jesus proclaimed the Good News, he said we needed to change our thinking so that we *could believe* that he was the Good News incarnate. Unfortunately, the Pharisees and so-called "experts in the law" refused to change their thinking, and so they couldn't see, and they couldn't believe.

So, why is this so important? Because, first of all, it's contrary to the Gospel (which we'll discuss in the next few chapters) and, second, trying to change my heart, ways, or behavior without changing the way I think, just doesn't work. It did not work for Israel (who kept sliding back into their sins), and it will not work for us either. In fact, this is why we need Jesus, why he came and died for us in the first place, and why we need to change our thinking.

So many people are stuck in their lives because of a misunderstanding of what it truly means to repent. And, yes, I'm talking even about authentic followers of Jesus. They made the decision to try this Christian "thang" out. Someone offered them FREE peace and joy, and they jumped at the opportunity. All they had to do was "accept Jesus as your savior." And so they did. Maybe that was you too. And as a result, you (they) felt a little better…a little more at peace…a little more content. However, nothing is really changing. Life is still pretty much the same ol' same ol' with some slight variation. You would not call it *transformation,* though…and neither would others who are watching you.

Maybe you're stuck in a relationship that you don't feel good about, or something feels wrong about how you're doing this relationship or the relationship itself. Maybe your family life is not improving – or your marriage. Maybe you're stuck in addiction. Maybe you're stuck in a financial pickle. You can't seem to make this Christianity thing work for you. You just can't seem to follow through. Why?

Were you being dishonest when you made the decision to follow Jesus? Were you insincere? I know a lot of people who are stuck (good friends), and I don't believe that they "didn't really mean it" when they decided to follow Jesus. In fact, I know lots of people *who love Jesus* but are still not being transformed. Again, I ask, "Why?"

First of all, nowhere in Scripture does it tell us that we need to "accept Jesus as our Savior." On the contrary, the Apostle Paul said this:

> *If you declare with your mouth, "Jesus is Lord," and believe in your heart that God raised him from the dead, you will be saved. For it is with your heart that you believe and are justified, and it is with your mouth that you profess your faith and are saved.*[11]

Confessing Jesus as my Lord involves a change of mind: *repentance.* If he is truly the Lord and master of my life and I truly want to follow him, then I must align my thinking with his. In other words, the problem is not that we choose Jesus and then change our minds when things get tough or we want what we want. On the contrary, it's that we choose Jesus *without ever changing our minds in the first place.*

In this day and age, letting the Bible change the way we think is rare. Instead of accepting and believing Scripture as truth, we have a tendency to read it like we're eating fish and picking through the bones. Those things we like or that don't stretch our faith too far we *add to* what we think we already know. However, those things that do not jive too well with our personal experience or history or politics we tend to qualify or redefine. So rather than changing our thinking about what is true and what is false, or what is right and what is wrong, we adjust *"our understanding"* of what Scripture *"must mean in today's culture"* so we can be more comfortable with it. This is why the pornography addict would most likely rather say, "I'm *struggling* with lust," than to admit the *whole* truth, which is: "I'm getting my butt kicked by my addiction to pornography." Relabeling my issue, however, does not change the truth about my issue, just as relabeling a container full of poison does not change its essence and make it any less deadly.

Case in point: today, it is socially acceptable for even followers of Jesus to believe that a person is "born" a homosexual. In other words, if I have feelings for someone of the same gender, "that's the way God made me." However, does that align with God's Word? Jesus declared that "No one is good—except God alone."[12] Does it make sense to you that this *good* God would create any of us gay or lesbian and then declare that homosexuality is sin (wrong)? Do *you* believe that God is like that? If so, you need to change your thinking about who God is and what he is like. Should any of us who are not good judge the only One who is? God created us for relationship with him. He did not create the obstacles that keep us *from* him. It was mankind's sin and disobedience that spawned those. However, *through Jesus,* we can overcome them no matter how overwhelming they might seem to be.

Let me be clear: I am not condemning people who are gay or lesbian. I understand why they would want to think that God made them that way. After all, who, in their right mind, would *choose* feelings that could potentially lead to a life of rejection and alienation. Similarly, I do not believe I really chose to be addicted to pornography. It chose me! My first encounter with pornography was not the result of me looking for it. In essence, I stumbled into it, and once I had tasted the forbidden fruit, I was hooked. I am not condemning anyone. No matter who we are or what we have done, God loves each one of us perfectly.

On the other hand, I am challenging what we have come to believe as truth because we are unwilling to change our thinking and align it with God's. Is the murderer born a murderer? Is the adulterer born an adulterer? Was I born already addicted to porn? No! It may not have been fair how I became addicted to porn. However, it is not God's fault nor what he wanted for me. On the contrary, he purchased my freedom and offered it to me as a free gift. However, before I was able to *realize* my freedom, I needed to change my thinking about some things.

Of course, this practice of relabeling things and thus conforming to our culture is not new at all. Here is how the Apostle Paul put it:

> *Do not conform to the pattern of this world, but be transformed by the renewing of your mind. Then you will be able to test and approve what God's will is—his good, pleasing and perfect will.*[13]

There it is in black and white. If we want to be transformed, we need to change our thinking and no longer go along to get along. In fact, according to this verse, if you do not align your thinking with God's, then you will not be able to figure out what God wants for you (what *"his good pleasing and perfect will"* is). Your own will and the will of an imperfect world is battling for top billing and God's will is being drowned out in the process.

We are products of our environment, and so is the way we think, whether we like it or not. So much of what we think or believe is programmed into us by our environment, our friends, and the world (kingdom) we live in. However, believers and followers of Jesus belong to a different kingdom, and if we are to follow that King, we need to align our thinking with his.

Do you want to be truly transformed? Do you want to truly be set free? The first step is changing the way you think – *repentance.* If you want God's blessings, you need to do things God's way and change your thinking about him – that he's perfect, that he's good, that he knows what he's doing, and that he is the same yesterday, today, and forever.[14] In addition, you need to change your thinking about *who you are* – that you're not all that (neither am I), that you don't know everything (neither do I), yet even though you don't deserve it (I neither), God loves you *perfectly*! And each of us needs to come to the place where we realize that when there's a debate about who is right and who is wrong, *God is the One who is always right!* Therefore, the question is, "Are you really following God, or are you expecting him to follow you?"

So, what does all this talk about repentance have to do with addiction and, in my case, an addiction to pornography? Most of the books written on the subject of lust or pornography (and I've read quite a few), or any addiction for that matter, focus on changing our behavior. However, when it comes to addiction, you can't "fake it till you make it." Even if you do learn how to control your behavior, it's still just control and not true freedom. This is why we relapse. And this is why we declare regularly, "Once an addict, always an addict."

However, God does not want to help us merely control our issues. He is not into building stronger cages for us. He wants to set us free! So, on one hand, the world (and even the church) was telling me that I could only learn to control my addiction. However, Jesus was telling me this: *"If you abide in my word, you are my disciples indeed. And you shall know the truth, and the truth shall make you free"*[15] and *"…if the Son makes you free, you shall be free indeed."*[16]

For years, I had believed what the so-called experts on addiction had told me: if I was going to be free from pornography, then I needed to confess everything to my wife, have an accountability partner, install better antipornography software on my laptop, etc. (i.e., build a stronger cage around me). If I was going to be free, I needed to change my behavior. However, I had done all that, and, even though I did not "struggle" as much, I still was not free. I still did not *feel* free. I knew I was going to fail again.

That is until I realized my freedom. The first thing was changing my thinking – and not just about this issue, but the very Gospel itself. After all, this is what Jesus instructed us to do: *"Repent, and believe in the gospel."*[17] So, what is *the Gospel*? That is what the next few chapters are all about.

4

Is Christianity Hard?

To be honest, my thinking (and understanding) changed about the Gospel (also called the "Good News") before my thinking changed about the issue of freedom from addiction. *It had to* if I was ever to realize my freedom. In fact, **even more than I had a pornography problem, I had a Gospel problem.** Gaining a proper understanding of the Gospel was foundational for my being able to even believe that true freedom was possible for me.

The beginning of the change in my thinking started with a question…

Some of the leaders, pastors (even I) at my church would often say this about the Gospel: "Christianity is so simple, but it's the hardest thing you'll ever do." Have you ever heard someone say that? Have you ever felt that way or said that yourself? Again, WE WERE WRONG! That may be difficult to swallow if you are struggling to live as a Christian as you read this. However, stay with me!

One day, as one of the leaders in our church droned this mantra in one of our services, a question formed in my mind: "What's so hard about it?" As I look back on it now and all that has happened since, I'm absolutely convinced that it was the Holy Spirit that whispered this question into my soul. In fact, that question began to haunt me. It was the itch that needed to be scratched. It drove me. I could not rest until I got an answer that made sense.

I began to ask every leader in our church this question: "We say all the time that following Christ (or Christianity) is so hard, but what's so hard about it?" Not one person gave me an answer that made any kind of sense. Addiction is hard whether you are a Christian or not. Trouble comes upon everyone whether you are a Christian or not. People you care about suffer and even die whether you are a Christian or not.

I have experienced many hardships in my life: rejection (including a broken engagement), losing loved ones to cancer (including my mom), losing pets (which are a BIG DEAL to my family because...well...they are part of the family), being sued by a friend...TWICE, not being able to get a job, drowning in debt, overcoming bankruptcy, etc. However, in every single case, I can honestly say, "It wasn't *worse* because I was a Christian." In fact, as a follower of Jesus, I have hope. I have hope that, someday, I will see my mom again. I have hope that, someday, when I finally meet Jesus face to face, *'He will wipe every tear from our eyes'* and, *"There will be no more death or mourning or crying or pain."*[1] Furthermore, people often come to Jesus when they are at the bottom of life. However, after choosing to serve Jesus, their circumstances improve as well as their joy, peace, and general wellbeing.

Some said, "What about persecution?" After all, both Jesus and Paul promised that, as followers of Jesus, we would have to endure persecution.[2] However, I was persecuted as a child for having red hair. In fact, when I was in high school while on the bus ride home, Laronda, an African American girl I grew up with, interrupted my daydream of actually driving to and from school in my own car, with this truth. "I feel sorry for you, Mel," Laronda began.

"Huh?" I countered back, "Why?"

Laronda continued, "Because, white people make fun of black people calling us all kinds of names. And black people make fun of white people calling them all kinds of names. But *everyone* makes fun of redheads!"

I didn't know whether to laugh or to cry. I chose to laugh because Laronda was my friend, and I knew she was just chiding me. However, she did make a good point that I had never really thought of until then. Of course, I am not insinuating in any way that my plight as a redhead was worse than or equal to Laronda's plight as an African

American. Still, to be picked on as a child because of the way you look, and which is beyond your control, is very alienating.

In my awkwardness of puberty, I was persecuted for having big feet and being a little chubby. As I grew up, some kids made fun of my nose which seemed to be growing faster than the rest of my face. Of course, if anyone commented about my nose, I would recall what comedian David Brenner said about his nose and counter with that: "I don't have a big nose. I have a small face."

You think you leave this kind of abuse behind when you become an adult, get married, and have kids, but then while driving together in the family car your first grader finds out your real name is not "Mel," but "Melvin," and he can't stop laughing. I took it like a man though. I pulled the car over and said, "Get out!" Of course, I was kidding...well...*mostly*.

Furthermore, let's be honest, although it is becoming less popular to be a Christian in America, we do not have to endure the kind of persecution that is happening in communist or Muslim countries and that many Christians must endure daily.

I needed to go outside of my usual surroundings if I was to find the answer to my question. And then an idea came to mind (again, the Holy Spirit? I believe so): "Call Daren and ask him."

Daren Lindley was a friend I had known for years though had not talked to in a while. Daren is the real deal when it comes to following Jesus "with all your heart and with all your soul and with all your mind and with all your strength."[3] Every time I have been with Daren, I have come away wanting to up the ante on loving Jesus. So, I called Daren, and after spending a few moments catching up, I said, "Daren, at my church people say all the time 'Christianity is so simple, but it's the hardest thing you'll ever do.' What's so hard about it?"

Daren did not even hesitate as he responded with this, *"Jesus said, 'Come to me, all you who are weary and burdened, and I will give you rest. Take my yoke upon you and learn from me, for I am gentle and humble in heart, and you will find rest for your souls. For my yoke is easy and my burden is light."*[4]

Daren continued, "Now the Greek word for easy means…[wait for it]…'easy.' And the Greek word for 'light' has the connotation of being so light it's '*uplifting*.' Daren was so right. The Greek word for "light" that Jesus uses here comes from a word that was used for how the wind drives the sails of a ship or how the wind drives the clouds. I guess Jesus truly is the "wind beneath my wings" (sorry, I couldn't resist).

As soon as Daren began to quote this passage, I began to laugh. How could I have missed this? How come I did not remember this? I knew this passage and had quoted it often from memory. Furthermore, why didn't anyone else remember this?

Nevertheless, here it was right in front of me in *red letters*. Although Jesus had declared that "Whoever wants to be my disciple must deny themselves and take up their cross daily and follow me,"[5] he also promised us that if we would go *all in* with him, his yoke would be easy, and his burden would be light.

So, this is what I concluded: life is hard for *everyone*, the law of God is *impossible* (and thus why we need Jesus), but following Jesus is *easy* (because Jesus said it is and makes it so). Not to say that there are not hard parts about being a Christian including dying to myself and living by faith (which we will address later in this book). However, walking with Jesus and *in freedom* are easy. And, if it's not easy for you (as getting free from addiction was not easy for me for so many years), then you are doing something wrong. Now, give me a chance to prove it and show you how God proved it to me.

5

What Is "the Gospel?"

If you had asked me a few years ago, "Mel, what's the Gospel?" I probably would have directed you towards 1 Corinthians 15:1-8:

> *Now, brothers and sisters, I want to remind you of the gospel I preached to you, which you received and on which you have taken your stand.* ***By this gospel you are saved****, if you hold firmly to the word I preached to you. Otherwise, you have believed in vain.*
>
> *For what I received I passed on to you as of first importance: that* ***Christ died for our sins according to the Scriptures, that he was buried, that he was raised on the third day according to the Scriptures, and that he appeared*** *to Cephas, and then to the Twelve. After that, he appeared to more than five hundred of the brothers and sisters at the same time, most of whom are still living, though some have fallen*

> *asleep. Then he appeared to James, then to all the apostles, and last of all he appeared to me also, as to one abnormally born.* [Emphasis mine]

Now to be sure, this is the Gospel. However, let me direct you back to something Jesus said at the very start of his public ministry and before any of the above even happened: "The time has come… The kingdom of God has come near. Repent and believe the good news."[1] Remember, "Good News" is the same as the "Gospel." Jesus begins by telling those listening that "the time has come" and "the kingdom of God has come near." Note, he does not say "will" come, or "will" come near. And because it is right in front of them in the person of Jesus (God come in the flesh) who is the Christ (or "Messiah," God's chosen One), they need to change their thinking (repent) and believe…RIGHT NOW! However, how can they believe in something that has not happened yet? Yes, the Kingdom of God has broken through and into their world through the person of Jesus. However, he has not died for them yet nor been resurrected from the dead.

The answer to that question is found in the meaning of the word "gospel." The word "gospel" comes from the Old English word "godspell" which means "good story." Every good story has the following: *who, what, where, when, why,* and *how*. The same is true for God's good story. In other words, the "Good News" Jesus is telling the people of Galilee to believe in is the "whole story." This, of course, includes the part they were witnessing that day, that is, the very words he was speaking to them and that he was the One the prophets foretold and that they had been waiting for. However, the "whole story" also included *everything* he was *going to say* and everything he was *going to do.* This too is what Jesus was calling them to believe in.

I just told you what the definition of the Old English word "gospel" is and which you will find in the King James or New King James versions of the Bible. And, although I prefer to read and study from modern translations (I don't speak Old English), I prefer to use this word "Gospel" over "Good News" for a couple of reasons. First of all, the Good News about Jesus is not like other good news. Also, the word "gospel" in Old English had this idea of *such good news* that it made you 'wanna' jump outta' your seat (like when my Seahawks won the Super Bowl). The Good News about Jesus is *that* good! On the other hand, the actual Greek word we translate "Good News," or "Gospel," is even grander than that!

The original Greek word that is translated to Gospel is not just "good tidings" but *such* good tidings that "sacrifices" and "thank offerings" are given because of this good news.[2] Think for a moment about your ultimate dream and desire of your heart. Of course, the bigger the dream and the higher the value, the more one would be willing to sacrifice to make that dream come true…right?

God's ultimate dream and the desire of his heart is to be reconciled with his creation (me and YOU). However, because of our sin, there was no possible way that unholy man could even be in the presence of a holy and perfect God...*unless, of course, God would make a way.* So, what was God willing to sacrifice for this dream? His very self. His very own Son, Jesus, would humble himself and become a man so he could die for our sins and then conquer the power of sin and death forever through his resurrection from the dead. This act of love would enable all those who would receive this free gift through faith to be clothed in his righteousness and holiness. This is the only way we can have access to a holy God.

This is the "Good Story." This is God's Story. And it is our story too if we want it to be. However, even this, as wonderful as it is, is not the whole story. THERE'S EVEN MORE!

6

Why the Gospel Is Easy

In Genesis 3, we read about the fall of mankind as well as the consequences for Adam and Eve's disobedience, which included their expulsion from paradise. Now to be clear, God did not boot them from the garden because he hated his creation and so he sent them to the corner for an extended timeout. On the contrary, God is love, has always been love, and will always be love. No, Adam and Eve had to be removed from his immediate presence because he is holy, and now *they* were not because of the stamp of sin upon their souls. And though God wanted to be close to his creation, this was no longer possible as his holiness would destroy them.

To be holy means to be "set apart." In God's case, he is set apart from us because he is perfect and we are not. This creates an impossible problem because holiness and unholiness cannot coexist in the same space. Here's the way the Apostle Paul put it: *"For what do righteousness and wickedness have in common? Or what fellowship can light have with darkness?"*[1] Furthermore, to a much younger pastor named Timothy, Paul wrote: "…God, the blessed and only Ruler, the King of kings and Lord of lords, who alone is immortal and *who lives in unapproachable light, whom no one has seen or can see*."[2] Why is God unapproachable? Because he is holy. Why can no one look upon him? Because he is holy.

Give or take, our sun is twenty-seven million degrees at the core and with a surface temperature of *only* ten million degrees. I say "only" in jest, of course, because if you or I were to even get close to the sun, we would be utterly consumed. Even if we were clothed in tungsten, which has the highest melting point (6177°F) of any known element in the universe, we would not stand a chance in the presence of the sun. Is this because the sun is mean? Of course not! It is because this is the sun's nature. The sun, by its nature, is unapproachable.

Now, let this next part sink in. The God that created that sun is described by the writer of Hebrews as "a consuming fire."[3] And, like the sun, he is not a consuming fire because he is mean but because this is his nature. He is so holy, so set apart from us, so perfect, and so unlike us in his perfection that unless he makes a way, we (because we too are stamped by sin) cannot get close to him without his nature consuming us.

This is why God, when asked by Moses if he would show him his glory[4] counters with, *"I will cause all my goodness to pass in front of you, and I will proclaim my name, the LORD, in your presence. I will have mercy on whom I will have mercy, and I will have compassion on whom I will have compassion. But...you cannot see my face, for no one may see me and live."*[5] In other words, God's glory (his holiness, which includes his goodness) would consume Moses. So, God simply gives Moses a glimpse that will not destroy him. Why? Because *"God is love."*[6]

Before their disobedience, Adam and Eve were able to sin but also able to *not* sin. However, with their disobedience, and because sin now had permanently tainted their souls and made them unholy, now they were *not* able *not* to sin. This also made Adam and Eve's offspring unholy as well (perpetuating the inability to not sin). This, of course, includes you and me. Try as we might...no matter who you are...no matter how good you think you are...it is impossible for every single one of us to live perfectly, and, therefore, to be holy enough not to be consumed by God's holiness if we were somehow allowed into his presence.

BUT, and here is the Good News, through faith in Jesus, we are made holy and righteous. In fact, here is what Paul wrote to the church in Ephesus:

> *Even before he made the world, God loved us and chose us in Christ to be holy and without fault in his eyes. God decided in advance to adopt us into his own family by bringing us to*

> *himself through Jesus Christ. This is what he wanted to do, and it gave him great pleasure.*[7]

And to the church in Rome, Paul wrote this:

> *We are made right with God by placing our faith in Jesus Christ. And this is true for everyone who believes, no matter who we are. For everyone has sinned; we all fall short of God's glorious standard. Yet God, with undeserved kindness, declares that we are righteous. He did this through Christ Jesus when he freed us from the penalty for our sins. For God presented Jesus as the sacrifice for sin...*[8]

Did you catch that? God loved us and chose us "to be holy and without fault in his eyes." Also, we are "made right" with God. Finally, God "declares that we are righteous." All of this is done "in" and "through Christ" as we place our faith and trust in him and what he has done for us. In other words, **we are not holy just in the times between our sins. On the contrary, for those who have put their faith in Christ, we are holy even when we are at our very worst.** This is so because our holiness is not dependent upon our own efforts and what we *do* (or don't do), but what Jesus has already *done* for us.

So not only are we able to draw close to God (even into "the most Holy Place"[9]), and the Holy Spirit is able to make his home in us, we are now through this same Spirit, once again, able to *not* sin. In fact, we are not only able to not sin, but we are *empowered* by God's indwelling Spirit to live a holy life. This is why Jesus's yoke is easy and why his burden is light – because it's his Spirit within us that is doing all the heavy lifting.

You and I may not be very good at forgiving others. However, God is very good at it, and he lives within us by his Spirit. We may not be very good at loving the unlovable. However, God is very good at it, and he lives within us. We may not be very good at resisting sin. However, God is very good at it, and he lives within in us. We are not very good at being holy. However, God is very good at it, and he lives within us. In fact, the reason why God is so good at doing all these things is because they are part of his nature. He can't help it! This is why Paul writes this to Timothy: *"…if we are faithless, he remains faithful, for he cannot disown himself."*[10]

The reason why Christianity is sooooooo hard for so many of us is that, frankly, we are doing it wrong. We are trying to do "our best" for Jesus. However, as my friend Daren Lindley shared with me that day I called him, **"Christianity is not doing my best for Jesus but Jesus doing his best in and through me."** It is "Christ in you" that is your hope in glory.[11] Not *you in you.* In other words, your freedom does not depend on your own ability but on Jesus's ability. Again, this is some Good News!

7

The Half-Truth 'gospel' Many Believe

Understanding the fact that God never changes (which is an aspect of his holiness) is key in realizing our freedom in Christ. At least it was for me and a huge part of my journey toward freedom. For if *"Jesus Christ is the same yesterday and today and forever"*[1] and *"God is love,"*[2] then how God feels about you and me is not dependent on how well we are doing at resisting sin.

I love the way J.D. Greear puts it in his book *GOSPEL: Recovering the Power that Made Christianity Revolutionary*. However, rather than quoting what he wrote exactly, I want to direct it toward you personally: ***'There is nothing you could ever do to make God love you more than he already does, and there is nothing you could do to make God love you less.'***[3]

In other words, God's love is like him; it's perfect! This means his love for us can't get better because it's already best. Furthermore, his love for us will never decrease or lessen either, no matter how much we mess up or fail God. No matter how bad you might feel about yourself right at this very moment, the fact is God loves you perfectly. And our sin (no matter how grievous) will not, cannot, ever alter that truth. Of course, I needed to own this, and so do you if want to realize your freedom.

This is where true repentance comes into play. We might have to change our thinking about the way God views us and feels about us. In other words, you don't have to "get your act together" so God will love you or love you more. God *cannot* love you more than he already does because his love is already maxed out. This means that when you are at your very worst, God's love for you is still the same: perfect. Now that is some Good News! However, this might be very difficult for many of us because we have been trained to believe a sort of half-truth gospel.

Although God does not change, we humans do (including us pastors), and because of this fact, the gospel we preach also changes, ebbing and flowing and reflecting more how we *feel* God feels about us rather than what is actually the truth according to the Bible. As a result, many of us (if not most of us) grew up hearing a mixed message about how God feels about us. On one hand, we hear how much he loves us *just as we are.* He loves us so much he even sent his one and only Son from heaven to walk among us and to die a cruel death upon a cross. On the other hand, we also hear (whether it is intentional or not) that we better get our act together, *or else!* And while it is true that God created us to do good works and is pleased with us when we follow him wholeheartedly, he doesn't love us any less if we don't. After all, he is our Father.

As an imperfect father of three sons, I do not love my boys (who are all young men now) any less when they mess up or don't measure up to my expectations of them. I love them no matter what! And that will never change. However, compared to God as our Father, I'm weak sauce. In fact, not only does his love for me as his son so surpass the love I have for my own sons, but his love for my sons also surpasses *my* love for them. That's right, God loves our children more than *we* love our children…because *his love* is perfect!

Please don't gloss over this fact. This is the kind of truth that sets you free.[4] God loves you no matter what! And that will never change. This means that if we do mess up, stumble, flat out fail, fall off the wagon or on our faces, we don't need to hide or run away, *because God loves us no matter what!* In fact, he has made a way to freedom, wants you to be free, declared that you are free (if he is your Lord), empowers you to be free through the Holy Spirit, and will help you realize that freedom as you continue to walk with him and follow him. He will never give up on you or abandon you[5] because he loves you NO MATTER WHAT!

Any voice that you hear that tells you something different than this originates from hell itself and our adversary, the devil. He accuses us and condemns us with his lies and half-truths. However, we overcome him by the blood of the Lamb, which covers us and washes us clean (no matter what we have done!), and our testimony, which is our agreement and alignment with Jesus and our declaration of our faith and trust in him.[6]

I believe the half-truths that we hear are the most dangerous. It is easier to see an outright lie for what it is. However, a half-truth can totally undermine our faith. In fact, I believe that many of us are stuck in one place because of our belief in a half-truth. And, in modern Christendom, there are many half-truths.

Half-truths are often very subtle. We believe these half-truths because they have *some* truth in them, seem very reasonable, and are often beneficial (or at least it *seems* that they are). However, there is a problem with half-truths. Here is what Jesus had to say about truth:

> *To the Jews who had believed him, Jesus said, "If you hold to my teaching, you are really my disciples.* ***Then you will know the truth, and the truth will set you free."***[7]

So, if the truth will set you free, what will a lie do? Isn't it obvious? It will keep you in bondage as a slave. This is true whether we are talking about a great big lie or just a little tiny one. That is why half-truths are so dangerous, because in reality, "A half-truth is a whole lie" (which is a Yiddish proverb).

This is why I believe half-truths originate from hell itself and the "father of lies," Satan.[8] In fact, Jesus said as much when he was teaching about both truth and freedom to both those whose hearts and minds were more open to him as well as those who were closeminded and whose hearts were hard. Satan does not want you to be free, my friend. If he cannot get you to reject Christ flat out, he will settle for trapping you in a half-truth. Either way, you're a slave, and he's got you right where he wants you.

We are not worthless sinners as I have heard many people say and, sadly, many pastors preach. This statement fits the bill of a half-truth being a whole lie. When Jesus says, *"So you also, when you have done everything you were told to do, should say, 'We are unworthy servants; we have only done our duty,'"*[9] he is not saying that we are worthless. A thing's worth is determined by what someone is willing to pay for it. When it comes to you and me, God purchased us with the death of his one and only Son. Therefore, and obviously, we are of great value to him.

Furthermore, our good works are not worthless either. Our good works have value, and God created us to do them. Also, they are evidence of the faith that resides within us.[10] They are only worthless in the context that they cannot pay for our sins nor make us holy and acceptable to God. It is kind of like trying to pay for goods and services in America with Canadian currency. Canadian currency has value in

Canada, but most places in America will not accept it. In the case of our sins, God does not accept our good works as currency for our sins. In fact, the only currency he does accept is perfection, which only he possesses. Of course, the Good News is that he gave his perfect Son in exchange for our sins. Why? Because he values us. Our creator deems that his creation was worth dying for.

Furthermore, when Paul says, *"Here is a trustworthy saying that deserves full acceptance: Christ Jesus came into the world to save sinners—of whom I am the worst,"*[11] he is not saying that we are all sinners, that he is the worst sinner of all, and that's just the way it's always going to be. This view totally flies in the face of what Paul also teaches us (*through the Holy Spirit*) about who we become in Christ. In fact, his point to Timothy in quoting this saying and attributing it to himself is that Jesus chose him to *"display his immense patience as an example for those who would believe in him and receive eternal life."*[12] In other words, if God can save and transform a horrible sinner like Paul, he can save and transform any one of us. In fact, this is what God does for all those who believe in him!

So, if we are not worthless sinners, then what are we? Here's the whole truth and nothin' but: we are saints! In fact, over sixty times (over forty times by the Apostle Paul alone) the New Testament calls believers in Jesus "saints." By the way, the definition of "saints" is "holy ones." Again, we are not holy because of anything we have done but because of what Jesus has done for us. God is the One who has set us apart, made us holy, and declared that we are righteous.[13] Of course, we must put our trust in him alone for this to apply to us as individuals.

If you are a saint, then this means that your sin *no longer* separates you from God, *even when you are sinning*. That our "sin separates us from God" is another half-truth which has been drummed into us for years and years. However, that statement *cannot be true* for those who have been made holy by Jesus's shed blood, his resurrection, and our faith in him. Sin separated us from God *before* we put our trust in Jesus, but not since.[14]

We may *feel* separated because of the guilt, shame, or conviction we are experiencing in the moment we are sinning or afterwards. However, our emotions often lie to us and cannot be trusted. Think of the times you have had a really bad dream or a nightmare. You wake up in a fit; your heart's beating, you are sweating profusely, and you are terrified. However, it was just a dream. It's not real, even though your emotions are telling you that it is.

Recently I had a nightmare, and our little Chiweenie (half Chihuahua, half Dachshund), Lulu, woke me up from it by licking me in the face. Obviously, she was worried about me, and so she rescued me from the lie I was trapped in. I don't know why I had the nightmare, nor can I remember what it was all about. Nevertheless, it sure *felt* real to me at the time. To be rescued from that nightmare was a huge relief. Furthermore, it may sound silly to some, but in that moment our sweet little Lulu rescued me, I didn't just feel relief – I also felt very loved. No matter who you are or what you have done, you too are loved *perfectly*, and it's time to wake up from some of the lies about who you truly are (and are not) in Christ.

Of course, we still sin. However, we are no longer "sinners" because God has declared that we are "saints!" Sure, we should still confess our sin as sin and ask God to forgive us. However, *that sin* is no longer something that is *between* the saint and Jesus. On the contrary, if you have been made holy by Jesus, then Jesus and you are on the same side of your sin and he is working in you, refining you, and transforming you. Remember, Jesus did not come to condemn you but to save you.[15] He is on your side! Right now, he has his arm around you, and he's whispering your name and telling you, "I got this! Let's take care of this thing *together*."

We cannot be both worthless sinners and saints at the same time nor does the Word of God ever say this. God is a God of order.[16] He is logical, not illogical. He does not talk out of both sides of his mouth. He does not play bait and switch. When Jesus says, *"Every kingdom divided against itself will be ruined, and every city or household divided against itself will not stand,"*[17] He is attempting to reason with the Pharisees so that they might see logic. Of course, the Pharisees were filled with pride, so instead of agreeing with Jesus by saying, "duh," they held on to their stubbornness. In other words, you cannot reason with someone who is *unreasonable*. Let us not be unreasonable when it comes to believing God and taking him at his Word, for he is not divided in any way.

So, what does all this have to do with addiction or struggling with any sin for that matter? Again, here's the truth and nothin' but: when Jesus declares, *"my yoke is easy and my burden is light,"*[18] that trumps whatever else we've been taught about how hard Christianity is. Furthermore, when Jesus declares *"…if the Son sets you free, you will be free indeed,"*[19] that trumps everything else you and I have been taught about the need to "battle" lust.

Paul said, *"Let God be true, and every human being a liar."*[20] In other words, God is the ultimate source of truth, and his Word is truth.[21] So, if Jesus (who is God) says, *"…if the Son sets you free, you will be free indeed,"*[22] you can take him at his Word. If Jesus is the Lord of your life, you are free! And not because *I* say you are, but because *Jesus* declared it. Not *sort of* free, or even *mostly* free, but *completely* free. Anything less than completely free is not really freedom. Of course, if you are not living free, then *you* have not *realized* your freedom yet. Your circumstances are keeping you from believing Jesus, just like they kept me from believing for so many years. After all, how can you or I be free if we keep messing up? Right? So, here is the issue and the verdict: If Jesus, the Truth Incarnate, says we are free, but we are not living free, then we are, in actuality, *living a half-truth.* This is why repentance (i.e., changing our thinking) is so important. Repentance enables us to cut through the lies and half-truths that are keeping us from taking Jesus at his word.

8

Discovering Faith

In the beginning of this book, I mentioned a class I had taught at our church called "Faith Discovery." As I mentioned earlier, this class was the result of a dream I had where I saw myself teaching a class for people who were just starting out on their faith journey in Christ, for people who were struggling to believe, and/or for people who had "lost their faith." Again, this class was based on the S.O.A.P. (Scripture, Observation, Application, and Prayer) model for reading the Bible so, in the class, we would examine passages about the importance of faith for the follower of Jesus, observe and discuss, make applications, and pray together. It was during one of our discussions that I had an epiphany moment where I realized "why" so many of us (including myself) stay stuck in addiction because we are believing and living a half-truth.

Of course, I would have never come to this new realization had I not already been on this journey to freedom that God had me on and had not my thinking already been changed about the Gospel and what it means to be a follower of Jesus.

The Greek word for disciple is *"mathetes"* which literally means "learner" or "pupil." However, a learner back then should not be confused with a learner in today's world. Students today learn all kinds of things. However, many (if not most) do so without ever even considering owning what they learn for themselves and assimilating it as part of their daily lives. In the ancient world, a disciple was a follower, apprentice, and adherent of his teacher and master. In other words, the goal for the disciple was to become like his teacher. In fact, the Scripture clearly shows this is the case for a disciple of Jesus: *"This is how we know we are in him [God]: Whoever claims to live in him [God] must live as Jesus did."*[1] So how did Jesus live then?

Many who read the above verse think in terms of just his obedience to the Father (and that's the near context of 1 John 2:5-6. However, the far and broad context of this verse is the entire letter of 1 John which includes faith and love as well. In fact, at the end of this particular letter John writes this: *"I write these things to you who believe in the name of the Son of God so that you may know you have eternal life."*[2] So, how do we know we have eternal life? It's simple, explains John – you reflect and resemble Jesus in your character: you believe in Jesus, you love others, and you obey God's commands. In fact, John repeats this theme throughout what we have come to know as 1 John.

As a follower of Jesus, I knew this well. Furthermore, to the best of my ability and through the power of the Holy Spirit, I had been living a life of faith, love, and obedience since I began following Jesus in the summer of 1981, my senior year of high school. On the other hand, my addiction to pornography, which began in middle school, still held me captive through most of my faith journey. However, on the first night of our Faith Discovery class, the Holy Spirit was going to show me why I hadn't realized my freedom as I walked our class around the bases of what it truly means to be a follower of Jesus. Let me explain what I mean.

Several years before, my wife, Denise, and I had planted a church in Nampa, ID. I was working as a speaker, entertainer, manager, and director for a company that performs academic and character development assemblies for elementary schools throughout America, Canada, England, and Australia. I had been with this company for almost twelve years and started as a speaker and entertainer. Through the vehicle of entertainment which included yo-yo tricks (that's right, I was a professional yo-yo man!), comedy, magic, and balloon art, I would capture the kids' attention that enabled me to encourage, challenge, and equip them with a motivational message. I had worked my way up in the company and was a director when both Denise and I began to feel God leading us back into vocational ministry after a long hiatus.

At first, we thought God was leading us to return to pastoring an existing church. However, through the course of time and many closed doors, we became convinced that he wanted us to plant a church. This was something neither of us wanted to do. However, saying "no, Lord" is an oxymoron Denise and I refuse to practice.

I had no clue what planting a church entailed, so I pulled up *Amazon.com* on my laptop and typed in "church planting for dummies" in the search bar. Seriously, I really did that, and obviously someone knew I was going to do this because *Amazon* gave me some suggestions. I bought a couple of books right then and there, read them, read a lot more books, and then we gave church planting our best college try.

Our church plant started out well enough. However, it eventually fizzled from lack of funds and the inability to secure a facility where we could meet on a regular basis. Yet I am just as sure now as I was then that this is what God wanted us to do even though it would be a failure (at least in terms of what man sees). I learned a lot from that "failure" about God, his faithfulness, myself, faith, pastoring, how to be a better leader, what not to do, etc. Furthermore, if I had gone to an existing church to be an associate or worship pastor, I would have most likely "done church" as I had in the past or in a manner following whomever I was working for. However, God had a different plan for me. God launched me into the unknown where I was so ill-equipped that it forced me to read, to learn, to step out of the box, and to lean on him. And this is what I did!

During that time, to help with the bills, I worked part-time as a hod carrier for my brother-in-law who is a gifted mason and who owns his own construction business. While driving home from the middle of Egypt (actually, I think it was Ririe, ID), I listened to an audio book entitled *Simple Church* by Thom S. Rainer and Eric Geiger.[3] In this book, Rainer contrasts growing and vibrant churches with those that have plateaued or are in decline. One of the common denominators (in fact, probably the most significant) of growing and vibrant churches is that they have a simple plan for producing and reproducing disciples. As I listened to this book, my heart grieved as I realized that our church plant was busy doing church but had no plan for making disciples. I pulled off the freeway into a rest stop and began to pray: "Lord, what do you want your disciples to look like?"

In that still small voice, he spoke to my heart, "I want the people you disciple to look like you: trusting, loving, obedient servants." Now to be clear, God was not telling me that I was to produce a bunch of mini Mels (one Mel is enough!). The Holy Spirit was simply reminding me that disciples should look like those who are leading them. The Apostle Paul reflects this model when he writes (under the inspiration and leading of the Holy Spirit) to the church in Corinth: *"Follow my example as I follow the example of Christ."*[4] Of course, this puts an incredible responsibility on the leader and the one doing the discipling.

This became the mission statement of our church-plant and is the mission statement of the church I pastor today: "Helping people become trusting, loving, obedient servants of Jesus." To help people remember what a disciple looks like, we developed a picture and a diagram. I loved baseball as a kid and played all the way into college, so it seemed only fitting to use a baseball diamond as our church's diagram. Even though not everyone plays baseball, it is the great American pastime, and most Americans know how baseball works. It's not a perfect analogy by any means. However, it works for us and is a useful tool in helping people understand what it means to be a follower of Jesus and how it is so vastly different from religion. So, let me take you around the bases that I took our Faith Discovery Class almost seven years ago.

Home Plate = Eternal Life

Just like in baseball, our model begins when someone steps up to the plate. Home plate is where the batter both starts and where he hopes to end up in that inning, thus scoring a run for his team. This is the goal in baseball: to score more runs than the other team and win the game. For followers of Jesus, what is our goal? Is it to go to heaven? A lot of people think and believe that. However, that's only part of the correct answer. Frankly, it's more of a *benefit* of being a follower of Jesus than the actual *goal*. Of course, God wants us to have "eternal life." However, Jesus describes "eternal life" not as a destination but in relational terms:

> [Jesus said] *"Now this is eternal life: that they **know** you, the only true God, and Jesus Christ, whom you have sent."*[5]

In other words, eternal life is not a destination but a personal relationship with a God who loves us. Like home plate in baseball, knowing God is both our starting place and our end goal. More than that, his has been *God's goal* from the very beginning: God wanted a people for his Name and a family that belonged to him. He created us for no other reason than to love us and that we might choose to love him as Paul so clearly communicates to the church in Ephesus:

> *Even before he made the world, God loved us and chose us in Christ to be holy and without fault in his eyes. God decided in advance to adopt us into his own family by bringing us to himself through Jesus Christ. This is what he wanted to do, and it gave him great pleasure.*[6]

This means that if you are a follower of Jesus, you have eternal life *right now* and not just when your body dies. This is true because eternal life (according to Jesus) is not a destination but a personal relationship with God the Father and with Jesus. In other words, because of his love, God made a way where we could not only have a personal relationship with him, but he also made that relationship of an everlasting nature.

First Base = Trust

Of course, the way we enter into this relationship with

God is through faith, which is first base for the follower of Jesus. In fact, this is how Paul explains the process of salvation to that same church in Ephesus:

> *For it is by grace you have been saved, through faith—and this is not from yourselves, it is the gift of God—not by works, so that no one can boast.*[7]

Religion is all about trying to get to God (heaven, paradise, etc.) through *doing* good things. However, as I've already illustrated, no amount of good things can ever change our flawed nature and make us holy. Here is where Christianity is radically different than anything else we call religion: We become holy not by what we *do* but through faith and trusting in what Jesus has already *done* for us. Again, this is Good News and the power of the Gospel.

Trust is another word for faith. I prefer using this word in this context because of its relational dynamic. After all, God does not want us to merely believe that he exists. This is why James writes to his fellow believers, *"You believe that there is one God. Good! Even the demons believe that – and shudder."*[8] The reason why the demons shudder is because they "know" God is real, yet at the same time they are outside of relationship with him. For the follower of Jesus, James contends, more is required than merely believing that God exists.

Trust is foundational in any meaningful relationship. And because that is what being a Jesus-follower is truly all about (i.e., a personal relationship with God), you cannot get to first base without it. In fact, the Scripture is clear that it is *impossible* to please God without faith and trust as the writer of Hebrews spells out:

> *And without faith it is impossible to please God, because anyone who comes to him must believe that he exists and that he rewards those who earnestly seek him.*[9]

The Word of God is adamant here that, yes, we need to believe God is real. However, we *also* need to believe that God is on the other end of our seeking. In fact, he is waiting for us and wanting to bless us. In other words, we need to believe that God is good and that he cares about us.

True biblical faith is not an abstract optimism that things are just gonna' work out. According to the writer of Hebrews, *"Faith is the **substance** of things hoped for, the evidence of things not seen."*[10] The kind of faith that pleases God is substantial (real, material, solid). It is not "blind faith" nor believing in things that are not *worthy* of trust. On the contrary, it is Jesus who is the substance of things hoped for! Jesus is real. He is tangible. He has got ahold of us and will never leave us or forsake us.[11] This is why so many have been willing to die for him through the centuries (and were faithful unto death!). In other words, their trust was in "Someone" and not just "something."

Faith is also limiting our options. Jesus said, *"In the same way, any of you who does not give up everything he has cannot be my disciple."*[12] You really have to trust someone before you will limit your options. This is why so many these days would rather not get married. They would rather not limit their options, or they do not trust the person they're living with enough to risk limiting their options. Giving up "everything" is not about Jesus wanting to ruin all of our fun but about trusting him and his direction for our lives. In fact, this is what Jesus is requiring from those who would choose to follow him.

Trust is the hardest part about being a follower of Jesus. However, if we can get to first base, then a miracle happens: God himself works within the believer to help him/her follow Jesus (as we have already discussed in the chapters about the Gospel). In fact, the indwelling of the Holy Spirit in the follower of Jesus propels us around the bases. This is how the Apostle Paul described it to the church in Philippi: *"...for it is God who works in you to will and to act in order to fulfill his good purpose."*[13] The Greek word for "work" here is *"energeo"* which is where we (obviously) get the English word "energy." In other words, God's Spirit is working in us, and he transforms both our desires and our actions. Again, this is why following Jesus is *easy*.

Second Base = Love

Being a follower of Jesus is not complicated. In fact, when Jesus was asked what the most important commandment in the Bible is, he said this:

> *"'Love the Lord your God with all your heart and with all your soul and with all your mind.' This is the first and*

greatest commandment. And the second is like it: 'Love your neighbor as yourself.' All the Law and the Prophets hang on these two commandments."[14]

Because being a follower of Jesus is first and foremost about a personal relationship with God, in order for that relationship to grow, we need to communicate with each other. This is why we pray and read the Bible. Prayer is simply talking to and with God. Through reading God's Word, God speaks to us. Of course, he can speak to our hearts as well. In fact, he can speak to us in many different ways. He speaks through the Bible, circumstances, others, dreams, nature, etc. One time God spoke to me through my son Caleb when he was just a boy.

It was 2009, the economy was a mess, and I couldn't seem to land a decent job to supplement my meager income as a church planter. In fact, we had gone from making almost six figures annually a couple years previous, to making less than 30,000. One particular day, I was letting my fear get the best of me. Actually, I was freaking out! As I walked through the house, I was praying and asking God if we were going to make it. As I stepped into the garage, I heard Caleb singing the song *Three Little Birds* by Bob Marley:

"Singin' don't worry 'bout a thing,
'Cause every little thing gonna be all right!"[15]

I do not believe this was a coincidence. When his critics told William Temple that his so-called "answers to prayer" were just coincidences, he responded, "When I pray, coincidences happen; when I don't, they don't."[16] When I heard Caleb singing that song, my heart filled with faith and I knew "every little thing gonna be all right" and it was!

Yes, God can and does speak to us in a variety of ways. He does so because he wants his sheep to hear his voice.[17] However, the clearest way to hear him is through his Word, the Bible. The Bible is not just another book. In fact, the Bible is "living and active" and able to divide the indivisible.[18] Because of this truth, I challenge you to read the Bible as God's side of the conversation. In fact, it is his love letter to us. If you read it, believe it, do it, and trust the kindness and the goodness of its most important Character, you will not only be transformed, but you will also grow to love this Author and Perfecter.[19]

Furthermore, being a follower of Jesus also means that I not only love God, but I allow his love to flow through me to others. However, it is not something I have to drum up or strive to do, but it actually flows out of my faith and relationship with God. Here is how the Apostle Paul described this truth to the church in Colossae:

> *We always thank God, the Father of our Lord Jesus Christ, when we pray for you, because we have heard of your faith in Christ Jesus and of the love you have for all God's people—the faith and love that* ***spring from the hope stored up for you in heaven*** *and about which you have already heard in the true message of the gospel that has come to you.*[20]

Again, we may not be very good at loving the unlovable. However, Jesus is very good at it, and he lives within in us through the Holy Spirit. And when we allow Jesus to love *through us,* it is a powerful testimony of God's power. This is what Jesus meant when he said, *"By this all men will know that you are my disciples, if you love one another."*[21]

Third Base = Obedience

For so many religions, obedience is the starting point. However, for followers of Jesus, obedience is third base. This is key in understanding the difference between religion and following Jesus. Jesus is not a religion. He is a person! He is God himself! Do not let your understanding of mythical gods color how you view Jesus as God. Jesus is not looking for you to appease God's wrath through good deeds or sacrifice. Jesus has *already* and *completely* taken care of all the requirements of the law through his own sacrifice and *completely* conquered sin *for us.* Our own meager efforts cannot add to what Jesus has *already* done for us, nor are they in anyway necessary. Only Jesus can make us righteous (i.e., "right with God").

> *"God made him who had no sin to be sin for us, so that in him we might become the righteousness of God."*[22]

What Jesus is wanting from us is relationship. And that relationship begins when we trust in what he has *already* done for us rather than trusting in ourselves and our own feeble works.

On the other hand, this does not mean that obedience or good works are not important. After all, James tells us that *"…faith by itself, if it is not accompanied by action, is dead."*[23] In fact, our obedience completes our faith. For example, if I say I trust God, yet my profession of faith never manifests itself in my choices and my behavior, then the truth is, I don't really trust God at all. I only say I do. Talk is cheap! John instructs us to put our money where our mouth is: *"Dear children, let us not love with words or speech but with actions and in truth."*[24] James drives this point home:

> *Do not merely listen to the word, and so deceive yourselves. Do what it says. Anyone who listens to the word but does not do what it says is like someone who looks at his face in a mirror and, after looking at himself, goes away and immediately forgets what he looks like. But whoever looks intently into the perfect law that gives freedom, and continues in it—not forgetting what they have heard, but doing it—they will be blessed in what they do.*[25]

So, if obedience is so important, why is it third base? Because if faith and love do not precede our obedience, it will taint both our view of God and our relationship with him. God is not looking for slaves. In fact, he has come to set the captive free.[26] Jesus is looking for followers who *want to* follow him, who *want to* serve him, and who love him. Motivation is everything!

Jesus said:

> *"If anyone loves me, he will obey my teaching. My Father will love him, and we will come to him and make our home with him. He who does not love me will not obey my teaching..."*[27]

When you read these words, how do you reflexively receive them? What do you think Jesus's tone is here? Is he saying, "If you love me, *show me*!" or is he saying something else? How you receive Jesus's words here all depends on how you view God and how well you understand the Gospel.

Unfortunately, many of us, because we have been so conditioned by religion, believe Jesus is saying, *"Prove it!"* As a result, we unwittingly jump onto a never-ending treadmill of good works to prove our worth. This is why so many give up on religion – because it's impossible to know when you've done enough. Again, our acceptability before God does not depend on anything we have done, are doing, or will ever do. Rather, it is based on what Jesus has *already* done for us.

On the other hand, the true follower of Jesus hears *"If anyone loves me, he will obey my teaching"* as matter of fact and so responds in his/her heart: "Of course I will obey because his Spirit lives within me, transforming me and propelling me onward; I can't help but obey, and, in fact, *I want to* obey and live a life that is pleasing to God."

So, what is the point of all the rules in the Bible then? I love the way JD Greear describes the purpose of God's law (the rules) as it relates to our relationship with God and its relationship to the Gospel: "The laws of God are like railroad tracks, pointing us in the direction to go… But those tracks do nothing to power the engine."[28] In other words, the law shows us what is right as well as God's will and what pleases him. However, there is no power in those commands to help us actually walk them out. Only the indwelling of the Holy Spirit through faith in Jesus gives the power to get down those tracks. This is the power of the Gospel! And this is why the Gospel is easy.

Remember Jesus is really good at loving people, forgiving people, serving, resisting sin (including pornography), obeying, etc. and HE LIVES WITHIN YOU if you've confessed him as YOUR Lord. Because of his great mercy and love for you, he has made us alive in Christ when we were dead in our transgressions.[29] That's right – before the Holy Spirit took up residence within us, we were dead men and women walking. Yet God's desire for us is that we might have eternal life with and in him.

I really love how Bob George, in his book *Classic Christianity* (which is a "classic" that everyone should read), likens this renewal process to canning.[30] Let me explain by using my own experience. When I was a kid, my mom used to can all kinds of things: pickles, green beans, peaches, apple sauce, apple butter, etc. My favorite thing she canned was blackberries and/or Marionberries. Her jam was awesome. However, I really loved it when she would make Marionberry pie. In fact, it's tied with sour cream lemon as my favorite pie to this day.

My mom canned with great care. After all, if you are not careful, it can be very dangerous, as botulism can be fatal. So, Mom would meticulously sterilize all the jars, lids, and seals. Of course, she did not do all this work just so we would have really clean Mason jars. Her plan was much bigger than this, and her goal was much joy for our family. Her plan was to put something really good in those jars, seal those contents inside, and preserve them.

The point of Jesus's crucifixion and death was to "do away" with our sins.[31] Consequently, when we put our trust in what Jesus has already done for us, it cleanses us…or, in keeping with the metaphor, it "sterilizes" us. However, this is not all Jesus has done for us. He did not go to all this effort and pain just we would be really clean vessels. His plan was so much bigger than this, and his goal was much joy for all who would believe in him and receive him. He made us clean so he could fill us with the Holy Spirit. By doing this, he made us alive by infusing us with his very self and his very life. In other words, as Bob George put it, 'Jesus did not come just to get us out of hell and into heaven; he came to get himself out of heaven and into us.'[31]

Because the Holy Spirit is in us, it should be easy to follow and obey Jesus. If it is not easy, then we are doing something wrong. It should be easy to say "no" to pornography. However, for me it was not easy. I knew all the right things and taught them, but for some reason I could not realize my freedom from pornography. I was doing something wrong, which the Holy Spirit would reveal to me right in the middle of this "Faith Discovery" class and as I was taking the class around third base.

9

My Epiphany

Up to this point in this book, I have been sharing my journey to freedom. However, I have also been building a foundation for you, the reader. It is the same foundation God had built in my life that positioned me to be able to take him at his Word. For if God hadn't shown me what true repentance really was, (that it's a changing of my thinking), and if he hadn't shown me what the Gospel really is (and that it's easy), and if he hadn't shown me the importance of faith (and that it is first base in the believer's life), then I doubt very much if I would have believed Jesus that night when he spoke to me and said, "Mel, you're already free. You just haven't realized it yet."

So, in a Karate-Kid-like fashion, it's been "wax on, wax off," "paint the fence," and "sand the floor."[1] My goal and my hope is that now *you* are in a position to believe for yourself and that my epiphany moment will become yours as well. So, here is how mine happened.

As we were rounding third base in our Faith Discovery Class, in an instant I saw how I was teaching one way (the right way) but living a wholly different way (the wrong way) when it came to my struggles with pornography (or any addiction for that matter).

I gave my life to Jesus the summer before my senior year in high school. I did not just stick my toe in either. I went all in! Truly, it was the best decision I have ever made. Because I was all in, when I was invited to join a Youth for Christ group, it was a no-brainer.

We did a lot of fun things that year in that group. The leaders (many of them teachers and coaches from my high school) were wonderful! To be honest, I do not remember what they taught us about Jesus or about being a Christian. However, I will never forget what they *showed* us through their lives. They showed us that being a follower of Jesus was life to the full! Every time we gathered was joyful, filled with laughs and abundant life. We played pranks on each other, we met professional athletes who shared their testimonies with us, and those wonderful leaders encouraged us and loved us *as we were* in all our imperfections.

One of my favorite things we ever did together happened in the summer right after I graduated. It would be the last time I would meet with this group. We had a picnic in Lewisville Park in Battle Ground, Washington. It was a beautiful sunshiny day! Besides sharing BBQ, we played softball together. However, our leaders added a twist to the game that made it hilarious! We played it backwards. If you were right-handed, then you had to throw left, and vice versa. If you batted right-handed, you had to bat left, and vice versa. You had to wear your mitt on your opposite hand as well. Finally, and most importantly, we had to run the bases in the opposite order. Instead of running to *first* first, you had to run to *third* first. The only person who got to do anything halfway normal was the pitcher, who was supplied by the team that was batting and who attempted to serve up a big fat pitch that the batter could hit easily. And these pitches would have been easy to hit if we were not hitting opposite handed. I cannot imagine how most of us could have hit anything if the pitcher was actually trying to strike us out.

This game was most hilarious for those of us who were actually decent baseball players. Quite a few of us had been playing baseball since we were kids, had played varsity baseball together on our high school team, and were on our way to college to play baseball there. Needless to say, we were conditioned to run the bases in a particular order, and it was totally foreign to us to run the bases in a backward order. So, here is what would happen to those of us who were so conditioned.

My fellow teammates and I could actually hit halfway decent opposite handed because we had practiced hitting this way from time to time just for fun. After all, we had all pretended, imagined, or dreamed that we were like Pete Rose or Eddie Murray (famous switch hitters in the big leagues at that time). However, we had *never* run the bases in backward order before. As a result, every one of us did exactly the same thing after we hit the ball: we *automatically* ran to first base. About half-way to first base, we would realize we were going the wrong way, so we would cut across the diamond to third. I think every single one of us baseball players did this…as well as laugh hysterically at ourselves when we did. We just could not help ourselves because we were so thoroughly conditioned to run to first base *first*.

Now back to our Faith Discovery class. As I mentioned earlier, we were rounding third when I remembered this backward softball game all those years ago. At that moment I realized while I had run to first base to come to Jesus and put my faith and trust in him, when it came to my addiction to pornography, I was trying to get free by running to third base *first*. The fact is, we all do this when it comes to addiction or sin habits in our lives, and I proved it to that class right then and there with this question: "When you mess up and fall back into sin in that usual area, what do you say to God?"

The hands went up from several, each one a unique individual with their own unique story. Yet all of their answers to my question were almost identical: "I tell God I'm sorry and that I'll never do it again (or at least try not to)." Is that what you *say* to God when you mess up and look at pornography? God showed me in that epiphany moment that that is what I had been doing for years. I had been trying to get free from pornography through obedience (third base), willpower, and guttin' it up. And why wouldn't I do that? After all, I had been so thoroughly conditioned by our culture, our twelve-step programs, our practices of accountability partners, and safe internet software applications. We have been conditioned to battle it out with sin through self-discipline and making covenants with our eyes (like Job said he did[2]). Some of us have found a measure of success in these efforts. However, we don't really feel free because, the fact is, it's not freedom. It's just a measure of control, and, like I explained in chapter two, control eventually leaks.

The Scripture is clear – the law is good. It both shows us our need for a Savior and *"until Christ came that we might be justified by faith,"* it has watched over God's people as a guardian.[3] However, it has no power to set us free! Scripture is very clear about this as we can see in Paul's letter to the Colossian church:

> *Since you died with Christ to the elemental spiritual forces of this world, why, as though you still belonged to the world, do you submit to its rules: "Do not handle! Do not taste! Do not touch!"? These rules, which have to do with things that are all destined to perish with use, are based on merely human commands and teachings.* ***Such regulations indeed have an appearance of wisdom****, with their self-imposed*

worship, their false humility and their harsh treatment of the body, ***but they lack any value in restraining sensual indulgence.***[4]

It is so ingrained in us that willpower is the solution to our addiction, we can't help but to automatically run to third base when we sin. We get that we are saved by grace, yet once we are saved, we try and live by the law. We just can't help ourselves. Again, I love the way JD Greear lays it out when he describes the Gospel:

"The gospel, however, is not just the diving board off of which we jump into the pool of Christianity; it is the pool itself. It is not only the way we begin in Christ; it is the way we grow in Christ."[5]

The amazing thing about this truth is that once you know it, you see the Gospel and the power of the Gospel *everywhere* as you read God's Word. It is not secret knowledge that only the learned and educated know about, *and unless they show us,* we will never see it and are lost. No! The liberating truth of the Gospel is not hidden at all but, as Paul writes to the church in Ephesus, made known for every single one of us:

"In reading this, then, you will be able to understand my insight into the mystery of Christ, which was not made known to people in other generations as it has now been revealed by the Spirit to God's holy apostles and prophets."[6]

In other words, it was a secret at one time. However,

now it has been revealed and shared openly and freely so that *everyone* will know *"the glorious riches of this mystery, which is Christ in you, the hope of glory."*[7] Why? Because God loves us and *"wants all people to be saved and to come to a knowledge of the truth."*[8] And because Jesus wants us to know the truth and be set free.[9] If this life-giving and shackle-breaking truth is hidden at all, it is hidden in plain sight and right in front of our noses. The reason we cannot see it is because we are trained not to see it.

You want more proof? When Jesus forgave, healed, or set someone free, what would he declare to them? Did he ever commend them for their hard work, willpower, self-effort, or adherence to the law? Of course not! On the contrary, over and over again, he declared matter-of-factly, *"your faith has healed you,"*[10] *"your faith has made you well,"*[11] or *"your faith has saved you."*[12] It was *their* faith in Jesus and his power that enabled the miraculous to break into their circumstance. Again, here is how the Apostle Paul puts it:

> *For in the gospel the righteousness of God is revealed—a righteousness that is by faith from first to last, just as it is written: "The righteous will live by faith."*[13]

Let me tell you a story. I am not sure if it's true, though it was told to me as if it was true. On the other hand, what this story illustrates is most definitely true.

Once upon a time the Dodgers were playing the Reds. The Dodgers were down by a run in the bottom of the ninth. With two outs and a runner on second, the great Maury

Wills stepped up to the plate in front of a packed and frenzied house.

Wills was not much of a long-ball hitter. However, he was probably the fastest man in baseball at that time, and all he needed was a single to tie the game and send it into extra innings. Mills, however, was not the type to settle for a single if he could stretch it into more.

Maury waited for the pitch he wanted and slammed it down the line. Not only would this tie the game, but with Wills' speed, it was a gimme triple. Furthermore, to add insult to injury for the Reds, the ball caromed off the wall in the corner awkwardly, keeping the outfielder from fielding it cleanly. Wills had already had an inside-the-park homerun in his career. Could this be number two?

As Mills full-steamed for third, the Dodgers' third base coach waved him home. It was going to be very close! Both Wills and the ball arrived at the plate almost simultaneously as a hush fell over the home crowd. Mills hook-slid away from the catcher's tag, and a cloud of dust plumed around home plate. As the dust settled, the umpire signaled safe, and the fans erupted! What an exciting and wonderful victory for the Dodgers! Or was it?

Not so fast! The Reds' first baseman was paying attention and noticed what most had missed, including the fleet-footed Wills. Maury had missed first base. The Reds appealed, and the first base ump, who was also paying attention, called Wills out. And because it was a force-out and the third out of the inning, the run that Maury had batted in would not count either. The Dodgers would lose, and the Reds would be victorious on this day.

Did this really happen? To be honest, I cannot find any proof of it. Preachers have been telling a story like it for many years. Same story, different players. However, there is no proof of *their* story either. Still, *this happens every day for followers of Jesus all over the world!* For the believer, first base is faith, trust, and surrender, and if we miss first base, we're out! And this is why so many of us stand on the outside looking in for our freedom.

For so many years, I had been trying to control my addiction through willpower, self-effort, 'tasting not,' 'touching not,' and 'handling not,' by attempting to make a covenant with my eyes (like so many books direct porno addicts to do), through having an accountability partner, through having an internet filter, through white knuckling it, by praying, and by 'just saying no.' Sound familiar? Yet in one epiphany moment, built upon a foundation that God had been laying in my thinking, the Holy Spirit opened my eyes to the truth, *and the truth set me free!* The way to my freedom could not be found by running to third base *first.* If I wanted to experience the freedom that Jesus had both promised me and declared to me, then I needed to run the bases in the correct order. I needed to believe!

So how did I put my faith into action and realize my freedom? I can't wait to show you, and by the way, it was *easy*!

10

~~My~~ OUR First Win!

So, one night I'm hearing Jesus speak to my heart, "Mel, you're already free," and the next day his Spirit is opening my eyes to the fact that I have been living the bulk of my Christian life, *not by faith*, but by works. I was playing the Christian life backwards. No wonder I wasn't realizing the freedom Jesus had promised me. However, now the path to victorious living was lit up like an airport runway before me: *If I wanted to walk in freedom, I needed to believe and take Jesus at his Word.*

I've heard it said many times that "there is no testimony without a test." My test would come before the week was through when, once again, I would stumble into temptation.

Denise had already turned in for the night. However, I

was still wired and not ready to hit the sack yet. As I was scrolling through the channels attempting to find something interesting to watch, temptation seized me! If you have ever been addicted to anything, you know what I am talking about. I was not out looking for a fight, but a fight had found me.

I believe the temptation came through one of those "FREE" previews of a premium movie channel. It might be free in the sense that it does not show up on your cable bill. However, it is not free when it comes to what certain movies do to your soul and especially when you are already a pornography addict and are unable to say, "No."

I did not know we were receiving the free preview or I could have steered clear altogether. Of course, this goes to show the futility of trying to completely shield ourselves from every possible temptation. In fact, I believe this is impossible. Yes, I could have chosen not to watch TV that night. And, yes, I could have chosen to go to bed with my wife instead of watching TV. And, yes, I could have chosen to read a book instead, or play a video game, or whatever. And, yes, we could have chosen not to have cable at all, or a TV for that matter. However, is that really freedom? I don't believe it is. In fact, it's just control. It's living in a cage.

So, there I was enjoying my "freedom" when a simple movie title (I don't remember what it was) caught me unaware. Curiosity is a powerful thing! In fact, I recall a men's retreat years ago where our speaker, Jack Hayford, showed us men that curiosity can be, as he described it, "a doorway to evil." Truly, curiosity can kill the cat, and it can kill you and me. In that moment, like many moments before, I was curious. After the wonderful week I had, I did not want to walk through that door. However, I did want to take *just a peek* through the keyhole. Of course, experience had taught me that if I said "yes" to the keyhole-peek, I would find myself pitching my tent on the other side of that door.

As I lingered at that "moment of truth," both excitement and fear gripped me simultaneously. Forbidden fruit by its very nature is exciting. If it wasn't, it would be easy to resist. The enemy of our souls teases us with the lie that we are missing out. This is how he tempted Eve (*and Adam* "who was with her") when she was being tempted[1] in the garden: *"For God knows that when you eat from it your eyes will be opened, and you will be **like God**, knowing good and evil."*[2] Furthermore, just like he lied to Eve saying, *"You will not certainly die,"*[3] he lies to us: "It doesn't hurt to peek"; "You're not ordering, you're just looking at the menu." He lies to us because he hates us. He wants to make us his slaves and to utterly destroy us. And all he needs to get his hooks into us is a little doubt or fear, a little envy, or a curious peek. It's like the old song from Doris Troy: "Just one look, and I fell so hard…Just one look, that's all it took."[4] This is why it's forbidden fruit; it's forbidden by a loving God because it is deadly poisonous and because it is also very addicting!

Of course, this was not my first rodeo. I had been at this crossroads before, and though the name of the cross street was different, its destination was the same dead end that I had driven to so many times before. However, it was not this realization that saved me. In other words, counting the cost did not save me, although it did give me enough pause to look before I leapt.

My heart was racing, but my mind was clear and weighing the truths that God had spoken to me that very week. Jesus had said, "Mel you're already free…" And even though my circumstances up to that point in my life were screaming the opposite, I decided to take Jesus at his word, and I declared this truth to the source of my temptation, the television set, that FREE preview, and the enemy of my soul: "No, I'm free." I did not yell it. I simply stated it matter-of-factly. And, just like that, a miracle happened! The temptation simply dissipated. It was still there, but its power over me was broken by my faith-declaration of divine truth: "I'm free!"

My heart no longer was racing. I was no longer wavering. I was *believing!* It wasn't me trying to control the situation or gut it up. I simply said the words, "No, I'm free." And, in fact, I felt free. I was *realizing* the freedom Jesus' had promised me. Like I said before, freedom 'oughta' feel free! It does, my friend, and it is wonderful!

It was easy too! It was easy because the Holy Spirit was doing the heavy lifting. I simply believed and declared what

Jesus had spoken to my heart and what Scripture clearly shows us. Through my faith-declaration, I had gotten out of the way and allowed Jesus to do his best *through* me.

This was my first real and *true* victory over temptation. Actually, it was *our* victory! Jesus had done the hard part by securing our victory over sin by his death and resurrection. I had simply said a few words in agreement of what he had already accomplished for all of us who believe and follow him. That was *our* first win. However, I have been enjoying victory ever since.

Of course, some might wonder, "Why didn't you try this before?" The answer is: "I never thought of it." I never thought to try it because I never thought it was an option available to me. I was preconditioned as an American Christian to believe that *I have to do something*. *I have to* go to a twelve-step program, or *I have to* have an accountability partner, or *I have to* have the right software on my computer, or *I have to* resist by fighting the urge, averting my eyes, taking a stand against temptation or sin, or taking a cold shower! However, like I have already mentioned, *"...these rules...indeed have an appearance of wisdom..., but they lack any value in restraining sensual indulgence."*[5]

It is kind of like what Abraham Maslow said; "I suppose it is tempting, if the only tool you have is a hammer, to treat everything as if it were a nail."[6] *The hammer (or the law) does not work when it comes to sin and temptation. However, the Gospel does work because Jesus already died for our sins, he already conquered sin and the grave, he already lives again, and we already live too and are already free (if we have put our trust in him). Yet, in order to release the power of that Gospel in our lives over our sin and temptation and experience that freedom, we have to take God at his word and stand on that word.*

11

Divine Power

Watch out for those dogs, those evildoers, those mutilators of the flesh. For it is we who are the circumcision, ***we who serve God by his Spirit****, who boast in Christ Jesus, and* ***who put no confidence in the flesh****...*[1]

The above Scripture is provided in the context of a reminder and a warning to the church in Philippi to not go back to thinking that their righteousness (and acceptability before God) is based on anything other than faith. However, it is also true that Christ-followers should have *"no confidence in the flesh"* for *LIVING* righteously as well. On the contrary, *"we...serve God by his Spirit."* In fact, to the church in Corinth, Paul writes this:

> *For though we live in the world, we do not wage war as the world does. The weapons we fight with are not the weapons of the world. On the contrary, they have divine power to*

demolish strongholds.[2]

Though unbeknownst to me at that time, when I squared off against my temptation and declared, "No, I'm free," those were not just mere words. On the contrary, I was drawing from the scabbard of God's Word, a weapon with divine power. If you take on a tank with just a stick, you're toast. The outcome is the same when we take on temptation with the *"weapons of the world."* Twelve-step programs, accountability partners, web filters, fighting the urge, averting our eyes, taking cold showers, and other forms of distraction have some value. However, at their core, they are merely *"weapons of the world"* and therefore lack any real power. This is why they don't and, in fact, *can't* set us free. They simply push the problem down the road, and the stronghold remains in our lives. Whether it is alcoholism, drug addiction, or some kind of sexual addiction, if you're still confessing that you're an addict after twelve months or twelve years, are you really free? In fact, doesn't your confession of "I'm an alcoholic" or "I'm an addict" clearly demonstrate that there is still a stronghold in your life? Of course, I don't need tell *you* that. Isn't that why you are reading this book in the first place?

So, what exactly are these weapons with divine power that we have at our disposal, and how do we use them? This is what this chapter and the next couple will focus on.

The Divine Power in Faith

We have already clearly identified one of these divine weapons as faith. Again, true biblical faith is not an abstract optimism in something simply working out. Of course, a person can choose to have a faith like that – and many do. However, there is no power in that kind of faith. For faith to have any power in it, it must be attached and invested in something substantial and full of power.

One of the attributes of God is that he is omnipotent. That means that he is not just *full* of power, but that he is *all-*powerful. There is nothing outside of his power, save that which is incongruent with his nature and character[3] (for example, God cannot ever do anything that is evil because, by his very nature, he is good[4]). God has power over gravity, time, sin, disease, Satan, and even death. This, of course, is why Jesus was able to heal the lame, cure leprosy, cast out demons, never sin, forgive sin, conquer sin, resurrect Lazarus *and himself,* ascend to heaven while his disciples looked on, and why he is eternal. AND when we put our trust in him, we gain access to HIS power. Knowing this, the Apostle Paul prays this for the church in Ephesus:

> *I pray that the eyes of your heart may be enlightened in order that you may know…his incomparably great power for us who believe. That power is the same as the mighty strength he exerted when he raised Christ from the dead and seated him at his right hand in the heavenly realms…*[5]

This is why, according to Jesus, we only need a

mustard-seed-size proportion of faith to move a mountain.[6] In actuality, it is not *our faith* that can move a mountain, but the *power of God* that our little faith taps into. I love the way Bob George puts it, "When you have a great God, you don't need a lot of faith – just enough to take him at his word."[7]

Consequently, this is why a royal official's son who was knocking on death's door was healed at the *exact time* when Jesus said to him, "Your son will live." Jesus, nor the father, needed proximity for this miracle to happen; after all, the man's son lay sick in Capernaum almost seventeen miles away. Neither did this "certain royal official" need *great faith,* for the Scripture is clear: he simply "took Jesus at his word and departed." By the way, this miracle led to not only him believing in Jesus, but "his whole household believed" as well.[8] This is what I am hoping for and praying for as I write this book – that my taking Jesus at his word when he told me I was free will also result in you believing and your freedom as well.

Of course, "what" exactly you are believing for also absolutely matters. Does it align with God's will? If it is not aligned with God's will, you can have all the faith in the world, but it just won't matter. This is probably why we don't see a lot of mountains thrown into the sea. A mountain thrown into the sea would be a cataclysmic and seismic event that would hurt an untold amount of people which God also loves deeply. On the other hand, believing that God would "move a mountain" of debt in your life as you put him first in your finances is totally possible. In fact, my wife and I have witnessed this personally in our own marriage and in the lives of many others.

Let me state it again – and with emphasis: **God is *all-powerful!*** Yet we have been convinced by our world (and, in fact, it has been ingrained in us) that while Jesus may have power over sin and death, he does not have power over addiction, and that's why we *need* twelve-step programs. Again, I am not knocking these programs. They do have *some* value. In fact, for those who don't believe and follow Jesus, it is their best chance to *control* their addiction. However, twelve-step programs are powerless to set us free because they rely on rules (the law) and human effort, and do not rely on Christ's power. Twelve-step programs might be good, but when it comes to true freedom, "good is the enemy of great."[9]

Whether your addiction is physical, mental, psychological, or spiritual, in every case it is simply a stronghold. Paul goes on to show that these strongholds are simply lies that we have believed and put our trust in. Therefore, he also writes this:

> *We demolish arguments and every pretension that sets itself up against the knowledge of God, and we take captive every thought to make it obedient to Christ.*[10]

So, what is the lie when it comes to addiction? It is this: that you *need* what you are addicted to; this is what it both *feels* like and *seems* like. Therefore, this is why it seems that you just can't say, "no" to your addiction. However, in truth, the addict is trapped by a lie, a stronghold, and as the Word of God states so clearly, *"The weapons we fight with…have divine power to demolish strongholds."*[11]

The Power of Jesus's Blood and Your Testimony

The blood of Jesus and your testimony, paired together, is another weapon with divine power. As part of a vision and visitation from an angel that God sent to the Apostle John and which was to be communicated to the churches of both that time and all time, John "heard a loud voice in heaven say"[12] this about the people of God:

> *They triumphed over him* [Satan]
> *by the blood of the Lamb*
> *and by the word of their testimony…*[13]

The "blood of the Lamb," of course, is the blood Jesus has *already* spilled for us and which has *already* purchased our freedom. Your "testimony," on the other hand, is your declaration of your trust in Jesus's completed work on your behalf.

For example, the night I truly realized my freedom when tempted by the not-so-free premium movie preview, the enemy of my soul was whispering his usual lie to me: "You know you need this!" And why wouldn't he use that lie when it had worked so well for him for all those years? However, *this time* the outcome would be different because, instead of just *resisting,* I parried his killing blow with my testimony of the truth: "No, I'm free." Again, I did not yell this but stated it matter-of-factly; it was not the tone of my statement but the truth in it, that made all the difference. Furthermore, my testimony was not centered in anything I had done but in the truth of what Jesus had spoken to my heart (and through his Word) and his blood shed for me.

My faith was tested, and since my faith was not in myself but in Jesus, it emerged from the fire even stronger. As result, I now had an even greater testimony. Consequently, this is why I have remained free ever since. Those divine weapons did not just give me a momentary victory but, as the Scripture promised, *"demolished,"* once for all, Satan's argument in my life! It was just as Jesus promised: *"Then you will know the truth, and the truth will set you free."*[14]

In the next chapter, we will take a look at yet another divine weapon that was key in my victory over my addiction.

12

The Power of HIS Words

When Paul concluded his letter to the church in Ephesus, he wrote this:

Finally, be strong in the Lord and in his mighty power. Put on the full armor of God, so that you can take your stand against the devil's schemes. For our struggle is not against flesh and blood, but against the rulers, against the authorities, against the powers of this dark world and against the spiritual forces of evil in the heavenly realms. Therefore put on the full armor of God, so that when the day of evil comes, you may be able to stand your ground, and after you have done everything, to stand. Stand firm then, with the belt of truth buckled around your waist, with the breastplate of righteousness in place, and with your feet fitted with the readiness that comes from the gospel of peace. In addition to all this, take up the shield of faith, with which you can

> *extinguish all the flaming arrows of the evil one. Take the helmet of salvation and the sword of the Spirit, which is the word of God.*
>
> *And pray in the Spirit on all occasions with all kinds of prayers and requests.*[1]

This is a very familiar passage in Christendom because it is regularly taught and preached about throughout the world. However, if our understanding of the armor of God does not rest on the foundation of the Gospel (which I've already explained), it's so easy to miss the true point of this passage as well as the divine power inherent in the armor of God.

Paul's teaching (again, inspired by the Holy Spirit) about the *"armor of God"* is a metaphor, and if we do not get that (as well as the power of the Gospel itself), we run the risk of missing the forest for the trees. In other words, we run the risk of focusing on the individual parts of the armor of God while missing what the Holy Spirit really wants us to know and understand.

I believe the point of this whole teaching is located in the first sentence: *"…be strong* ***in the Lord*** *and* ***in his mighty power."***[2] After all, it is the devil himself and his schemes and spiritual forces of evil that oppose us. Our strength and our power are not sufficient in battling such powerful opposition. However, everything we need for victory is ***"in the Lord."*** It is not our own version of truth or our own righteousness that can save us. On the contrary, Jesus is *"the truth"*[3] and is our righteousness.[4] Also, he is our peace[5] and the Prince of Peace[6] (in other words, God owns peace). He is also our hope and salvation. It is our faith "in him" that extinguishes the flaming arrows of the evil one. Furthermore, *"the word **of** God"*[7] is our sword. Finally, we are to pray not just in our strength but *"**in** the Spirit."*[8] In other words, our victory is *"in"* the Lord. Without him, we have already lost. Again, this is why so many of our efforts against addiction are futile – because they are centered in human effort and not *"in the Lord."*

Since I have already addressed at length the power of the *"shield of faith"* in previous chapters, it is not necessary for me to belabor that point in this chapter (though it is definitely worth repeating as it was so key in my own victory). On the other hand, I feel compelled to both encourage and challenge you to pick your shield up off the ground and begin to use it; in fact, never let go of it! After all, you cannot win the battle against *"the devil's schemes"* without it.

In this chapter, I want to specifically focus on *"the sword of the Spirit, which is the word of God."*[9] This divine weapon was also key to my freedom, though I did not realize it until months later.

The word that Paul uses here when speaking of the *"word of God"* and which we translate *"word"* is the Greek word *rhema.* I will not pretend to be an expert in Greek though I have been trained in the proper use of Greek-English tools. Using one of those tools, we see that *rhema* means simply (in this case), "any sound produced by a voice and having a definite meaning."[10] In other words, when Paul says, *"the word of God,"* in this instance, he is referring to the actual words of God and the words spoken by him. Of course, this would also apply to the words of God as spoken through the prophets as well as any and all of the truths revealed by the writers of Scripture *"as they were carried along by the Holy Spirit."*[11] Finally, because Jesus is God, *all* of his words are the words of God as well. Contrary to what I have heard and read and that some teach, *rhema* does not mean "the instant, personal speaking of God to us." I mention this because you may have been taught this as well. So, let me repeat: the *rhema* of God does not have to be "instant" nor "personal" to you. It simply means that it comes from God and that it has a definite meaning.

Make no mistake, God's words have power! They are not just mere words. On the contrary, as it states so clearly in Hebrews...

> *...the word of God is living and active, and sharper than any two-edged sword, even penetrating as far as the division of soul and spirit, of both joints and marrow, and able to judge the thoughts and intentions of the heart.*[12]

Out of nothing, God created the world with just his words. God said, *"Let there be light,"* and there was light.[13] Of course, he didn't stop there. He kept talking, and, over and over, "it was so."[14] With just his words, Jesus calmed the seas, cast out demons, and healed the sick. With just words, God does the impossible. Of course, when they are God's words, they are never "just" words. On the contrary, God's words are infused with divine power!

Consider Jesus and how he battled temptation. Immediately after Jesus is baptized in water in the Jordan River by John the Baptist, Jesus, *"full of the Holy Spirit,"* is led by the Spirit into the wilderness.[15] There, in the wilderness, Jesus would eat nothing and would be tempted by the devil (Satan) for forty days.[16] All alone and hungry, Jesus would face the forces of hell that would converge on him and prey upon his humanness. Satan would throw everything, including the kitchen sink, at Jesus, attempting to compromise his integrity and his holiness. Satan's weapon of choice would be half-truths. As the *"father of lies,"*[17] this was something Satan was very skilled at. In fact, it had worked so well with the first Adam, why wouldn't it work with the last Adam as well?[18]

Satan's first swipe attempts to exploit Jesus's very real hunger. So, he says to Jesus, *"If you are the Son of God, tell this stone to become bread."*[19] No doubt, the idea of eating fresh bread would be very appealing and very tempting to any man who has not eaten for forty days. And, make no mistake, Jesus, though fully God, is also fully man and, therefore, is as hungry as you or I would be after starving ourselves for that long. And, although Jesus could tell stones to become bread, he also recognizes that it would be wrong for him to do so in this case because he would be buying into the lie that Satan was selling here: that we *need* to feed our appetites and our hungers. This is the same lie Satan feeds to every addict: "You *need* something to take the edge off"; "You just *need* to get through the day"; "You *need* to be fulfilled sexually"; "You *deserve* to be happy."

Jesus, however, recognizes the subtle lie and counters Satan's argument with the Sword of the Spirit. God has already spoken the truth on this issue, and it has already been written down. However, in order for the power of this truth to be released, Jesus has to speak it and declare it to the temptation itself and the source of the lie, Satan himself. A sword is merely decoration as long as it is in its scabbard. It does not become a deadly weapon until it is unsheathed and engaged in combat. This is, in effect, what Jesus does when he answers the adversary thus:

> *"It is written: 'Man shall not live on bread alone.'"*[20]

In fact, Jesus is quoting from Deuteronomy 8, which says this:

> *He humbled you, causing you to hunger and then feeding you with manna, which neither you nor your ancestors had known, to teach you that man does not live on bread alone but on every word that comes from the mouth of the* LORD. *Your clothes did not wear out and your feet did not swell during these forty years.*[21]

In other words, God, and not mere bread, is our sustenance. As human beings, we do not *need* anything so much that we would have a reason to compromise ourselves to get it.

Furthermore, anything that we might need, God will provide as we put our trust in him and seek him first in our lives.[22] As quick as it began, this part of the battle is over as Satan's half-truth is unmasked and his argument is demolished. However, Satan is not ready to throw in the towel just yet.

Satan aims higher and offers Jesus a much bigger prize. He promises to give Jesus authority over all the kingdoms of this world. However, Jesus rebuts the temptation for immediate power because he is not looking to rule over us but to *redeem us* from sin and death. There is no shortcut to that goal. The way of the cross is the only way. In fact, if he bows to Satan, he will actually undermine the will of God. No, God's way is God's will. Therefore, Jesus responds, *"It is written: "Worship the Lord your God and serve him only."*[23]

Finally, Satan tempts Jesus to prove himself as the Son of God by leading him to Jerusalem, having him stand on the highest point of the temple, and suggesting he jump. After all, Satan cajoles, *"For it is written:*

> *"'He will command his angels concerning you*
> *to guard you carefully;*
> *they will lift you up in their hands,*
> *so that you will not strike your foot against a stone.'"*[24]

Satan does not misquote Psalm 91 here, but he does misapply it in the attempt to, once again, manipulate Jesus into compromising his holiness. One little sin will do, and Jesus will no longer be the unblemished Lamb. He will no longer be worthy. He will no longer be able to substitute himself for us, satisfy our debt, and cover our sins *"once for all."*[25]

However, once again, Jesus sees through the ruse because he not only knows the verse Satan misapplies, he also knows the context, and he knows that, *"It is also written: 'Do not put the Lord your God to the test.'"*[26] Game, set, match! Class dismissed! The devil's fiery darts do not even leave a dent because Jesus knows the truth. In effect, Satan has been disarmed because every lie is diffused by the truth. As a result, Satan has had enough and vacates the premises.

I want you to understand something about this example from Jesus's experience: **truth is just as powerful in our hands as his.** The words of God are powerful because they are absolute truth that slash through any and every lie. Furthermore, the same Spirit that empowered Jesus in the wilderness resides in us who believe. Do *you* believe? Have you put your trust in Jesus? Then pick up your sword (which is the Word of God), and pick up your shield (of faith), and prepare for battle! The fact is the battle has already been won by Jesus, and the victory is already yours. However, you need to declare it! Speak it out loud. Speak it to both the lie and to the liar: "No, I'm free!"

13

The Power of Being in Jesus

In the beginning was the Word, and the Word was with God, and the Word was God. He was with God in the beginning. Through him all things were made; without him nothing was made that has been made. In him was life, and that life was the light of all mankind. The light shines in the darkness, and the darkness has not overcome it…

The Word became flesh and made his dwelling among us. We have seen his glory, the glory of the one and only Son, who came from the Father, full of grace and truth…

No one has ever seen God, but the one and only Son, who is himself God and is in closest relationship with the Father, has made him known.[1]

The word that Paul uses in Ephesians 6 (*rhema*) is different than the one that John uses when he writes, *"In the beginning was the* ***Word****, and the* ***Word*** *was with God, and the* ***Word*** *was God."*[2] The word John uses here is the

Greek word *Logos* (pronounced "LAH-gahss"). Some teach that this word (*logos*) refers to the "written word of God." However, this is obviously not what John is trying to convey here. When John writes *"In the beginning was the Word,"* he is not saying that "in the beginning was *the Bible*." On the contrary, we can see clearly from the context of John 1 that John is writing about *Jesus*. Furthermore, he clearly shows that Jesus was not only sent by God, but that he is, in fact, God, Creator, and all-powerful.

So, why does John refer to Jesus as "the *Logos*" then? To understand this, we need to recognize the original audience to which John was writing and with whom he was sharing the Good News. While some think John was writing to a varied audience of Jews and gentiles (anyone not Jewish), others believe he was writing to a mostly gentile audience. However, it does not really matter because both Jews and gentiles lived in a Greek world. In fact, the common language of the day was Koine Greek (which literally means "common Greek"). The Jews may not have believed in the gods and philosophy of the Greeks, but they knew what the Greeks believed and what they worshiped. They couldn't help but know because that was the world in which they lived.

Of course, John's goal (with the Holy Spirit guiding him) is to share Jesus with them in such a way so that they not only understand who Jesus truly is but that they also *believe* in him. So, John starts with where they are and establishes common ground by referring to Jesus as "the

Logos."

Around five hundred years before Jesus came to earth as a man, there was a Greek philosopher by the name of Heraclitus. During his lifetime, Heraclitus introduced an explanation of our world that many still believe today, although the terms that Heraclitus used to describe his worldview have long passed out of use. Heraclitus described the constantly changing and chaotic world (the *kosmos* or *cosmos*) that we see and live in as "*flux*" (not to be confused with Emmett Brown's flux capacitor in *Back to the Future*[3]). However, behind the *flux*, Heraclitus believed and taught, was an order, structure, or formula that held everything together and which was its opposite. He called this hidden structure or formula "the *Logos*." Furthermore, Heraclitus taught that this *Logos* was common to all but difficult to know and impossible to comprehend.[4] Of course, through the course of time, languages do change, and the word *logos* came to mean "word, speech, or discourse." However, in John's world (i.e., the *Hellenistic* world) what Heraclitus taught was common knowledge.

As in John's day, many believe today that there might be a god, but they also believe he is like the Wizard of Oz; if he exists at all, it is behind the scenes. However, this god really does not care and therefore allows bad things to happen. Furthermore, he is impossible to know.

It is these kinds of unbelievers that I believe John addresses, and he states absolutely that there really is a

Logos. In other words, something behind the curtain really exists and has existed forever. In fact, this something is really a *Someone* who was not only with God but is God. He is the Creator of everything. In him is life, which he has given to mankind because he is good and all-powerful. In fact, the darkness cannot hold a candle to him nor stop him in anyway. Furthermore, he loves us so much that he makes himself known to us through the person of Jesus.

In this same Gospel of John, we see another picture of Jesus speaking to those who had believed in him:

> *"If you continue in my word, then you are truly my disciples; and you will know the truth, and the truth will set you free."*[5]

The Greek word Jesus uses here is also *logos*. Because Jesus uses this word specifically (and not *rhema*), I wonder if Jesus is telling his disciples not just to continue in his *words*, but to continue to embrace him in *relationship*. Doesn't this make sense in light of Jesus's words in John 15:5? Read it for yourself:

> *"I am the vine, you are the branches; the one who remains in Me, and I in him bears much fruit, for apart from Me you can do nothing."*

And doesn't this mirror Paul's words in Ephesians 6:10 when he instructs us to *"...be strong* ***in the Lord****..."*? The point I am trying to make is that the power of the Gospel flows out of *being in* Jesus rather than just *doing* Christlike things. As I mentioned before, being a Christian is not about doing your best for Jesus but Jesus doing his best in and through you.

These are the weapons we fight with (or should be): *"the sword of the Spirit, which is the Word of God"*[6] (His Words! His truth!); the shield of faith (believing what Jesus says to us and about us rather than our circumstances); the blood of the Lamb, which covers us *once for all,* making us holy (this is our testimony!); and Jesus himself who indwells us and empowers us through his Spirit. These weapons are infused with divine power and, in fact, are God himself battling for us and who has already triumphed over the enemy through Jesus. These weapons are giant killers and dragon slayers. They're smarter than smart bombs and more penetrating than bunker busters.

Why would any sane person settle for a peashooter when they have access to this arsenal? Yet that is what so many of we addicts do and are trained to do. This is what I did for so many years. However, God took me on a journey and walked me into his armory, and like Neo in the Matrix, *I began to believe.*[7] And, though it might have started as or seemed like a *lucky shot* when I first declared that I am free (though I'm absolutely certain luck had nothing to do with it), I am now well-versed in handling these divine weapons, am very accurate, and I use them with much intentionality. Furthermore, and let me be clear, it is not a struggle for me to do this. Using God's weapons are as second nature to me and as natural as breathing. I am not striving to live in freedom as I once strived to resist temptation and sin through the use of those *human* weapons (cold showers, accountability partners, etc.) that addicts are trained to use.

Recently, my son Chase (whose testimony and journey you'll get to read later on) was having a conversation with a friend about pornography. We'll call this friend Bob for the sake of confidentiality. (To be honest, I don't even know his name because Chase didn't share it with me – only the story.) Bob was sharing with Chase how he had struggled *before* with pornography but was now doing well through the use of these "human weapons" we've described. Through the course of the conversation Chase could tell that Bob wasn't really experiencing freedom but that he had only attempted to build himself a better and stronger cage. And even though Chase challenged his thinking over this issue with Scriptures that clearly argued otherwise (like the ones I've clearly laid out in this book), Bob refused to bend in any way. Bob's mind was made up. However, Chase could see trouble ahead for his friend because he recognized that Bob was trying to talk himself into being free rather than truly living free. Like I said, Chase cares about his friends, so he asked Bob a question, "Bob, do you *feel* free? After all, shouldn't freedom *feel* free?" Bob was caught by the truth and admitted that he did not feel free.

My friend, freedom truly does feel just as it ought to…FREE! I'm not striving, because I'm FREE! I'm not striving, because God's truth has set me FREE! Of course, the truth is that I was free the moment Jesus set me free all those decades ago when I first put my trust in him as a senior in high school, because *"...if the Son sets you free, you will be free indeed."*[8] The problem was I did not believe I was free. My perspective was a tunnel-view through prison bars. However, the rest of my cell was demolished, and I could simply walk out if I chose to. And I *would* have walked out except that a lie had kept me staring straight ahead, oblivious to my already-bought-and-paid-for freedom. The lie was that I was an addict, a prisoner of addiction that simply could not say "no." This lie argued and pretended that I was the opposite of what Jesus said I was, and I believed that lie, so I kept staring through those bars hoping one day I would be free. However, like I said, God took me on a journey and woke me up to the truth. He shined a light into that sweatbox I called home and exposed my addiction for what it truly was – a lie! And once a lie is dismantled by the truth, it no longer has power over you.

> *For though we live in the world, we do not wage war as the world does. The weapons we fight with are not the weapons of the world. On the contrary, they have divine power to demolish strongholds. We demolish arguments and every pretension that sets itself up against the knowledge of God, and we take captive every thought to make it obedient to Christ.*[9]

14

Sympathy or VICTORY?

I believe one of the deepest cries of our hearts is to be understood. This is especially true for the addict. We are more than our addiction. Our stories are complicated and so varied. When we were kids, none of us were dreaming and hoping that one day we would be slaves to addiction and sin. On the contrary, we were dreaming of being professional athletes, firemen, policemen, soldiers, doctors, lawyers, etc. However, our enemy (who, make no mistake is very real!), exploited our pain and weakness and trapped us in a lie. We may not have gone looking for our addiction. Nonetheless, it has indeed found us and enslaved us.

Part of the allure of a twelve-step program for the addict (if we can get past actually admitting that we have a problem) is that it is a safe environment where others understand what you're going through and truly sympathize with you. This communal understanding and sympathy is valuable and helpful in the healing of your heart. Furthermore, the group keeps you from lying to yourself about your addiction. On the other hand, there is also an inherent danger in these kinds of communities. Rather than gaining control, healing, or freedom from their addiction, addicts sometimes settle for simply receiving sympathy. In fact, it becomes their new *substance* that they get addicted to.

I was no exception to this rule. Remember, pornography (or any addiction for that matter) is simply a symptom of a deeper problem. As a young man, my heart had been broken by a tremendous amount of rejection. I medicated that pain by indulging in pornography. Through pornography, I was able to fantasize about a woman who would not reject me but actually say "yes" to me. When my wife would say "no" to me, my still-wounded heart would interpret that as *more* rejection. Pornography, again, would grant me an escape from what I *felt* was reality. Through the course of time, however, God would heal my heart through the truth of his Word. What I was *feeling* was actually a lie I was *believing*. The truth was that God loved me *perfectly*! Believing and embracing this truth would eventually also change how I viewed my wife's love for me. Please understand though, that some of the greatest healing in my heart in this area came *after* I had already realized my freedom from pornography. I didn't have to be completely healed to walk in freedom, and neither do you. Complete healing and wholeness is also a journey.

Turn back the clock with me, if you will, to when I was a young Christian man and the wound in my heart was bleeding profusely and I couldn't grasp why God wouldn't just deliver me from my addiction. I was living in this secret world and very much thought I was alone until I read this from the Apostle Paul himself…

We know that the law is spiritual; but I am unspiritual, sold as a slave to sin. I do not understand what I do. For what I want to do I do not do, but what I hate I do…

…For I have the desire to do what is good, but I cannot carry it out. For I do not do the good I want to do, but the evil I do not want to do—this I keep on doing. Now if I do what I do not want to do, it is no longer I who do it, but it is sin living in me that does it. So I find this law at work: Although I want to do good, evil is right there with me. For in my inner being I delight in God's law; but I see another law at work in me, waging war against the law of my mind and making me a prisoner of the law of sin at work within me.[1]

Needless to say, I was encouraged. In fact, at the time, I wondered if Paul struggled with lust just like I did. This is how badly I longed to be understood. I just wanted some sympathy and to feel like I was not "the only Christian who was stuck." It is like the old adage, "Misery loves company." So true!

If this is where you are, I totally empathize with you.

You are not alone! In fact, according to a nation-wide study by the *Barna Group* conducted in 2016, "47 percent of men and 12 percent of women in general seek out porn at least once or twice a month."[2] However, for teens and those under twenty-five, those numbers increase significantly with 33 percent of women and 67 percent of men acknowledging that they seek out porn on a monthly basis.[3] Furthermore, *Barna* also reported that, "Most pastors (57%) and youth pastors (64%) admit they have struggled with porn, either currently or in the past."[4] Like I said, you are not alone! Not by a long shot! On the other hand, while sympathy might make us feel better, it will not lead to victory!

In my experience as a pastor, I have come to the realization – and not because I want to, but because that is just the way it seems to be – that many people really do not *want* to be healed or free. When I say "healed," I am not really talking about physical pain, though that can certainly apply. Mostly, I am talking about being healed and set free from their past.

Many *say* they want to get better. However, it seems that their pain has become their best bud. They love to talk about their friend. In fact, in the house of their life, they have given their pal a room of their own. Their pain is not just a friend. It is part of the family. If their "dawg" moved out and skipped town, they would be undone. What would they talk about? WHO would they talk about?

This reminds me of an encounter Jesus had with a man who had made friends with his infirmity.[5] We are not really sure what that infirmity was, but apparently it slowed him down quite a bit and confined him to a mat. Was he paralyzed? Maybe. The Scripture is not clear, though. However, he had been *"ill"* for 38 years.[6] That is a long time to get to know someone and get buddy-buddy.

So, when Jesus comes to Bethesda Memorial Swimming Pool, where this guy is hanging out, and asks him, *"Do you want to get well?"*[7] the man does not really know how to answer. No one ever asked him that before. No doubt, many had asked him *what* happened to him or *how* it happened to him or *how long* he had been like this or *"is there any truth to the rumor about an angel stirring the water from time to time and whoever dives in first gets healed?"*[8] He was a pro at answering those questions. However, no one had ever asked him if he wanted to get well before. That's a dumb question! Duh! That's why he was there in the first place…*because he believed the rumor and wanted to get well.* Right?

Then why doesn't he say to Jesus, *"Yeah, I would really like to get well"*? Maybe he did not really know who this guy was who was talking to him or about all the people he had healed already or that he was the Great Physician and God in the flesh. And while that may be true, it still does not explain his answer, *"Sir…I have no one to help me into the pool when the water is stirred. While I am trying to get in, someone else goes down ahead of me."*[9] Do you see it? More than he wanted to be made well, he wanted to tell Jesus about his friend, *Max Pain.* **He wanted sympathy, not victory.**

This is what I wanted when I read Romans 7:14-23 for the first time. I wanted sympathy. I wanted freedom too. However, the volume of the cry of my wounded heart would drown out the liberating truth of what Paul was actually teaching. I had missed Paul's point entirely as many do when they read this passage. The reason why is because the "heart wants what the heart wants," and we human beings tend to hear, see, and believe what we *want* to hear, see, and believe. As a result, we do not see, hear, and believe what we *need* to hear, see, and believe in order to be healed and set free.

I love what Greg Koukle habitually says when asked questions about the Bible, he responds: "Never [just] read a Bible verse." He goes on to say, "Instead, always read a paragraph at least."[10] This is not to say that the truth of a single verse cannot stand on its own. However, we should always make sure that what we *think* the verse says is what the original writer (again, carried along by the Holy Spirit) is *actually saying.* My associate pastor and best friend, Brian Ellingson (who briefly shares his own journey to freedom later in this book), loves to say, "Use the 20/20 rule." In other words, read the twenty verses before the verse in question, and read the twenty verses after.

The problem with the popular interpretation of this passage (i.e., that Paul is struggling with sin) is that it does not take into account everything Paul has written before Romans 7 and everything afterwards (especially Romans 6 and Romans 8). *Romans* is a *letter* written by Paul to believers in Jesus who live in Rome. Although it is to and for us as well as part of God's Word, it is still a letter. Therefore, when *we* read it, we should also read it just as we would read any letter and not chop it up into bits and parts.

The reason we can know that Romans 7:14-23 is not Paul divulging a secret struggle with sin is because of what he says in the rest of the letter. In the previous chapter, Paul declares that, as believers in Christ, we are no longer slaves to sin[11] and sin is no longer our master.[12] Furthermore, "though you used to be slaves to sin…you have been set free from sin and have become slaves to righteousness,"[13] and "now you have been set free and have become slaves of God."[14] Is Paul (God's mouthpiece to not only the Christians in Rome but to us as well) talking out of both sides of his mouth? Of course not.

So, what does Paul mean then when he says, "I have the desire to do what is good, but I cannot carry it out"[15]? First of all, we know from Romans 7:1 that Paul is speaking to followers of Jesus "who know the law." Furthermore, we also know from Romans 1:6 that these Roman believers are also Gentiles. Unlike the Jews, they did not grow up learning the law. However, they know it now and are probably having a hard time understanding the relation of the law to their new faith in Jesus. So, Paul tells them clearly that they are "not under the law but under grace."[16]

I became a follower of Jesus the summer before my senior year in high school. I will never forget that day when Pastor Daniel Westerfield, at a small church in Camas, Washington, shared that it was Jesus who was "a friend who sticks closer than a brother."[17] I so desperately wanted a friend like that, and I gave my heart, soul, and mind fully to Jesus that very moment.

As a boy I believed in God and prayed to him often, mostly from the on-deck circle of a Little League Baseball field and while waiting for my turn at the plate. As I grew up, I came to understand (and believe) that Jesus had died for mankind and that he was raised from the dead. However, it was not *until* I realized that Jesus loved *me* and wanted to have a personal relationship with *me* that I put my trust in him.

I was a pretty good kid. I did not do drugs or alcohol or sleep around (though I could not say "no" to pornography), I was a straight A student, and I obeyed my parents. In other words, I did not think there was much I needed to be saved from. However, at the moment that I said "yes" to Jesus in my heart, I felt the most incredible and freeing sensation as my sins were literally being lifted from me. It was at that moment I truly realized how bad I was and how good God was. Like I said, I went *all in* and have never looked back. I asked for a Living Bible for that very next Christmas (because the King James Version was "Greek to me"). I am not sure if it was my favorite gift that year, but it is the only one I can remember. That very Christmas day, I began to read five chapters every night before I went to sleep. If I missed a day, I would read ten chapters the next night. I thought this was what Christians were supposed to do. There was only one problem with my new discipline: I started in the Old Testament and with the book of Genesis. I started with *the Law.* I was very independent (actually very insecure and filled with pride) as a young man, so I wasn't about to ask someone where I should start reading in my new Bible. I read it like any other book; I started at the beginning.

By the summer, I had read through the whole Old Testament. In the fall, I went to Concordia College in Portland, Oregon. I was there on a baseball and an academic scholarship, though I also received financial aid because my family was poor. I was excited to begin my first year and especially excited about my very first Bible class: *History and Literature of the Old Testament*. By the end of that class, I had now read through the Old Testament (and *the Law*) twice and barely any of the New Testament. Like the Roman believers, I too was a Gentile, and I too knew the law. I had entered into the Kingdom of God by faith. However, most of what I knew was the Old Covenant and the Law. I had yet to read and come to know what the New Covenant (OUR covenant!) was really all about. And, like the Romans, I did not truly understand the relation between the Law and my actual standing in Christ. As a result, I leaned on my own self-effort rather than the grace of God and the Holy Spirit.

For a new believer in the days of the early church, it was a lot easier to learn the Law than the New Covenant. The Law and the Prophets had already been written down, and you could learn all about them by visiting your local synagogue, even if you were a Gentile (though you could not actually sit with the Jews). On the other hand, the New Testament was *being written* as the Gospel writers shared their testimonies about Jesus and as Paul, Peter, John, James, and Jude wrote letters to the churches.

Therefore, it makes total sense that many new believers (whether Jew or Gentile) would err on the side of the Law rather than on the side of grace. Besides that, it is just human nature to rely on self-effort and "the rules." So, Paul instructs the Roman believers clearly in the purpose of the law and that being under grace is not a license to sin.[17] Paul explains to them (and to us) the law no longer has authority over them because they have died to the law in Christ.[18] Instead, we now live by the Spirt of God.[19] That does not mean that the law is bad. Its purpose was to show us our sin and our need for God, and it has accomplished that purpose.[20] In a sense, it is kind of like an X-ray or MRI. Both of these are good. These tools show our doctors what is wrong with us so they can properly diagnose our condition and prescribe the right treatment so we can get well. However, these machines do not cause the condition. They just show us what is already there. Furthermore, these machines cannot heal us either. They are not designed to.

With different illustrations, Paul is showing us the same thing about the law.

One of the illustrations Paul uses is from his own life and his own futile attempt to obey God by and through the law and through self-effort. The reason we get confused here is that Paul describes his own story in present tense as if it is happening right now. However, it's just an illustration through which Paul is passionately trying to drive this point home: *the law is good, but it cannot save us.* We need the Great Physician! And, in fact, Jesus has *already* conquered sin through his death and resurrection and served up the cure to all those who believe. Therefore, Paul declares, "Who will rescue me from this body that is subject to death? Thanks be to Jesus Christ our Lord!"[21] Paul is not talking about a future day when Christ "will" set him free. On the contrary, he is reliving the moment when he realized his own freedom in Christ. How can we know this for certain? Just keep reading…

> *Therefore, there is **now** no condemnation for those who are **in Christ Jesus**, because through Christ Jesus the law of the Spirit who gives life **has set you free from the law of sin and death**. For what the law was powerless to do because it was weakened by the flesh, God did by sending his own Son in the likeness of sinful flesh to be a sin offering. And so he condemned sin in the flesh, in order that the righteous requirement of the law might be fully met in us, who do not live according to the flesh but according to the Spirit.*[22]

On the other hand, if we continue to live according to the law (as many of us do, and especially Christian addicts), we will struggle just like Paul did before he embraced Christ, died to the law, and began to walk and live in the Spirit *through faith*. Paul wants this same freedom for us. Life in the Spirit is the path forward. Do not go back to that futile way of living – riding the fence and wavering between realms.

> *You, however, are not in the realm of the flesh but are in the realm of the Spirit, if indeed the Spirit of God lives in you. And if anyone does not have the Spirit of Christ, they do not belong to Christ. But if Christ is in you, then even though your body is subject to death because of sin, the Spirit gives life because of righteousness. And if the Spirit of him who raised Jesus from the dead is living in you, he who raised Christ from the dead will also give life to your mortal bodies because of his Spirit who lives in you.*[23]

I want to be honest with you. It was not until I really understood the Gospel and realized my freedom that I truly understood what Paul was actually saying in Romans 7. The fact is there are a lot of people who frankly just do not want to see the truth. They love the law and self-effort too much (whether they realize it or not), and, therefore, they have a hard time understanding their *new* position in Christ. Remember, the Old Testament is not our covenant. Ours is the New Covenant! Those unwilling to become new wineskins[24] will never be able to see how truly *easy* living for Jesus can be. So many would rather settle for sympathy than to live in victory.

What do you want, my friend? Do you want victory, or do you want sympathy? I'm guessing that you want victory, or you probably would have quit reading a long time ago. Do you want to get well and live free, or would you rather just talk about your sidekick? **Here is the truth:** ***you cannot have both!*** **For if you get victory, your homie has to move out. There is no place for them anymore because Jesus is moving into that room (and every room).** And instead of a sob story, you now have a testimony. Instead of you being the victim, Jesus is your hero!

Praise Jesus! He has won the victory, and we too are more than conquerors in Christ![25] It is your choice, though. The fact is you will never really realize your own freedom until you truly want to. You have to want it! And if you are not sure you have come to that place yet where you truly want it, then do this: pray and ask God to cause this desire to grow in your heart until it's absolute. Remember, if you are a believer, he lives in you. This is what he wants for you. This is his will for you. In other words, this is an easy prayer for him to answer.

Choose victory today!

15

"Show Me – Sand the Floor..."

So, we have finally reached the part of the book where I tell you what to do so you can begin to realize your own freedom, right? WRONG! This book is not about giving addicts another thing (or *step*) "to do." A methodology cannot set you free. If it could, it would have already, and you would not be reading this book. If I give you something *to do,* I exacerbate the problem because I steep you back into the law and the curse that comes from leaning on the law.[1] Building a stronger cage (i.e., the law) is not the remedy, and we need to resist the temptation to solve our issues by asserting that there is a rule we can follow. Let me say it again, and in no uncertain terms – *faith is the answer!*[2] In fact, you already know what to do if you have been absorbing the truths as I have laid them out in this book, and you are believing the Word of God about who you are and what God says about you.

Recently, my wife, Denise, and I spent some time with my sister and her husband, Julie and Jon Carter, in Nampa, ID. Our good friends (and associate pastors at our church), Brian and Iris Ellingson, were also with us. As we drove to dinner together one evening, I was quizzing my sister about her church (Awaken Church in Nampa, ID) that she and Jon were thriving in as they were helping couples restore their marriages and realize their freedom in Christ. I had heard their pastor, Adam Cooke, speak online during our COVID-19 "isolation" and immediately loved his heart, message, and vision. One of the things I was curious about was how well they were growing. I was blown away to discover that they were growing like gangbusters *through the pandemic* and with a relatively young African American leader at the helm in a part of the country which is less than one percent African American – which goes to show that love, grace, truth, and a focus on Jesus conquers racial division on any given day of the week and twice on Sundays.

Of course, my next question was, "Do you guys do any advertising, or is it pretty much all word-of-mouth growth?"

"Ya know," Julie responded, "In the church we used to be in, our pastor would always tell us that we needed to invite people to church, but hardly anyone did. However, Pastor Adam doesn't tell us to invite people, and almost everyone does. He says all the time, 'When you know who you are, you'll know what to do.' And he focuses on telling us who we are."

"When you know who you are, you'll know what to do."

Ever since Julie told me this, I cannot get that statement, *that truth,* out of my mind. In fact, as I look back over my life, I realize now that this is what God was doing in me all along; he was changing my thinking about who I am – and who I am to *him*.

Our society (we pastors included) loves to focus on symptoms. Since they are the most obvious, they get our most immediate attention. They are what we *see* and what we *feel*. However, if you really want to get well, you need to get to the root cause of your condition. I believe that for every single one of us the root cause of what's gone wrong in our lives is a lie that we believed when our heart was scarred or wounded: "I'm unacceptable," "I'm just a sinner," "This is all I'll ever be," "I'm all alone," "I don't have what it takes," "I'm insignificant," "I don't matter," "I'm not enough," "I'm useless," "I'm worthless," etc. This *"message feels final and true, absolutely true,"* John Eldridge explains, *"because it's delivered with such force."*[3] Most often, this devastating wound, or offense, assaults us when we are young and in our formative years and we begin to believe its corresponding message at that time, and we believe it with all of our hearts. Furthermore, these lies are often compounded and reinforced throughout our lives as the scab gets picked, and further hurts remind us of our already wounded heart.

For me, this wound first occurred in little league baseball as a result of being bullied. No doubt my bullies picked on me because of their own insecurities, and pushing me down somehow made them feel better about themselves. Unfortunately, my bullies had some influence and could gather a crowd around them and convince the crowd to join in with them in their persecution of Mel Steinmeyer. When I made the all-star team when I was fourteen and one of them did not, they fabricated a story that I was selected only because my dad was a coach and, more specifically, the coach of the all-star team that year (because our team had won first place in our league). The truth was that while I was selected by coaches' vote (and not the popular vote of the players), at that coaches' meeting, my dad never even brought up my name, nor did he vote for me. In fact, he explained to me that it was not necessary for him to chime in at all because all of the other coaches were unanimous that I should be on the team. My dad wanted me to know this that very night of the coaches' selection meeting because he loved me and believed in me and did not want me to doubt myself nor my ability.

Still, my dad was aware of how the continuing jeers were affecting me and thought it might be better *for me* if he did not start me in our first game. However, his assistant coach (who was probably the most respected coach in our whole little league) insisted that I start and bat second in the order. I so desperately wanted to prove myself to these doubters, and in our first game, I was able to do so. Our team was annihilated by the heir apparent, Evergreen Little League. However, I was able to leg out three of our four hits in that game. Regardless, the jeers continued.

Next year, I would try out for the high school team, and as I walked past the busses that were going home for the day (i.e., minus the students participating in afterschool activities), another kid (not one of the bullies but one of my own *teammates* on our championship team) yelled out the window, "Steinmeyer, you don't really think you can make it, do you?" and he laughed. I remember others laughing with him as well. My response was a hesitant, "We'll see."

I made that team when many of my all-star teammates did not (or did not have the courage to even try). I thought *now* I had proved myself and *now* they would respect me. However, the jeers and the doubts would continue. As a result, I would believe a message, a lie, that I just did not have what it takes, and I would become driven to prove that I did. And even when I received a baseball scholarship to play baseball at an NAIA school, I still was driven to prove myself. In other words, my worth as a man became tied to whether (or not) I could prove myself, my ability, and/or my worth.

In college, when I was hitting over .300 and playing flawless defense, I received limited playing time behind another freshman who was not playing as well but continually started ahead of me. The scab on my heart was picked again. A couple years later, after surrendering my scholarship to attend Bible college and in the midst of a pastoral internship at a very large church, the senior pastor of that church would actually say the words, "Does this guy have what it takes?" (Not as a question but as an indictment). Needless to say, my wound was ripped wide open once again.

Over and over in my life, I would hear this message in so many different ways. When I couldn't change my freshman football coaches' minds about me no matter how well I played, my heart could hear them say, "Steinmeyer, you don't have what it takes." When girls would reject me: "Mel, you don't have what it takes." When I would get into a little fender-bender the very first day I drove my new 1966 Ford Galaxy to school (well, it was new to me): "Face it, Mel, you don't have what it takes." When I was the top student in both Physics and Honors Math IV and yet the Math and Science Award was given to another student who had the same classes but who scored lower than I: "Mel, if the very top score is not enough, you definitely will *never* have what it takes." When another church wanted to hire me to work full-time but was only willing to pay me an intern's salary with no benefits: "Mel, you're not worth the money; you don't have what it takes." When my fiancée broke up with me: "SORRY, HONEY, YOU DON'T HAVE WHAT IT TAKES!!!" When I couldn't keep up with managing two departments at my work and then was demoted: "Do I have to spell it out for you? Y-o-u d-o-n-'-t h-a-v-e w-h-a-t i-t t-ak-e-s!" When our church plant failed: "I know. I don't have what it takes." When our church would struggle to grow or gain momentum: "Yeah, yeah, I get it. I don't have what it takes." And every time someone would leave our church, I would hear that same ol' familiar jingle ring in my soul: "Mel, you just don't have what it takes, and you never will." He's a little slow, folks, but he finally catches on.

Now turn the clock forward. For thirty-seven years I had failed to prove that I have what it takes to control my addiction and my lust. For me, the message and the lie that I had first heard and believed when I was a kid had become my reality: "I guess I don't have what it takes." Consequently, you could tell me all day long to just stop (or start) doing something. However, until I quit believing the lie that had shackled me, I couldn't stop. I couldn't stop because it was who I was…or at least, it was who I *believed* I was.

Unfortunately, most books and remedies concerning addiction focus on behavior modification and *controlling* our urges. This is only *Band-Aid* therapy and therefore ineffectual at truly setting us free. As I have already mentioned (and at length), *been there, done that!* However, God took me on a journey that was not about showing me what to do but who I truly am and who I am to *him*. I believe this is what Paul means when he writes to Titus, *"For the grace of God has appeared that offers salvation to all people. It teaches us to say 'No' to ungodliness and worldly passions, and to live self-controlled, upright and godly lives in this present age…"*[4] Did you catch that? It is the *"**grace** of God…*[that] *teaches us to say "No" to ungodliness and worldly passions…"* I have read this passage so many times, and, in fact, I have even memorized it. However, its truth had eluded me until this past year. It was God's grace that had taught me to say "No." It was not the law, or a twelve-step program, or a prescription I read in a book about addiction. All along, it was God's grace training me and showing me the way. In fact, God's grace was showing me who I truly am in Christ:

> I am not unacceptable. In Christ I have been made holy.[5]
>
> I am not a sinner. I am a new creation[6] and a saint.[7]
>
> This is not all there is or all I am. For *"He who began a good work in you will carry it on to completion until the day of Christ Jesus."*[8]
>
> I am not insignificant. God has chosen me.[9]
>
> I am never alone. Jesus will never leave me nor forsake me.[10]
>
> I am not insufficient. I can do all things *through Christ* who gives me strength.[11]
>
> I am not lacking. He has given me everything for life and godliness.[12]
>
> I am not useless. I am *God's handiwork* and gifted by the Holy Spirit to do good works.[13]

I am not worthless. In fact, he has purchased me with his very own blood.[14]

I am not a slave because he has set me free![15]

This is who I am. God, who does not lie, says so.

For years, I believed a lie: I was a slave (after all, isn't that what addiction is – slavery to some substance or habit?). While I may have gotten a little better at controlling my addiction to pornography (or at least the space in between my indiscretions grew a little), ultimately, I would fall because I knew I would fall. Circumstances and the wound in my heart – that I didn't have what it takes – had convinced me that this was the truth. So, this is what I believed. This is who I was and would be until Jesus finally took me home to be with him.

However, although I might give up on myself, God would never give up on me! Nor will he ever give up on you, my friend. And just as Jesus whispered to me, "Mel, you're already free. You just haven't realized it yet," he whispers the same to you through this book and my story. Are *you* ready take him at his Word?

Those words are no less powerful because they are repeated. After all, isn't it true that Jesus was repeating himself when he spoke those words to me? After all, he clearly stated this truth two thousand years ago when he said, *"…if the Son sets you free, you will be free indeed"*?[16] This, in fact, is how I knew that it was Jesus who was speaking to me that night (and not my own mind making something up) because I had already read and knew his words from Scripture. However, I needed to take him at his word and believe that truth and that it was *for me.* That night, I began to believe, and, in an instant, the stronghold that was so firmly established in my life and that had kept me imprisoned for so long began to crumble around me. Now it is your turn to begin to believe.

Let me remind you one more time of what happened just a few days later. As I was scrolling through channels, that familiar temptation seized me once again. However, this time was different. This time I knew who I was, and so I said so out loud: "No, I'm free." Remember, I did not yell it. I just simply stated it matter-of-factly to the TV set, the temptation, and the enemy of my soul. The outcome was that the power of the temptation (the lie) dissipated and fizzled. It was still there, but it had no power over me now. Its power had been extinguished by my faith in Someone who is *all-powerful* and by his Word which is living and active and which penetrates to the core and divides the indivisible.[17] No one told me what to do that night. Because I finally knew who I was "in Christ" (and believed it!), I *instinctively* knew what to do.

It was like I was a Danielson squaring off against Mr. Miyagi.[18] I thought I was sanding the floor. However, I was really learning that true repentance was changing my thinking. I thought I was waxing a car. However, I was really learning that following Jesus was easy because God's

Spirit was within me and doing all the heavy lifting. I thought I was painting a fence. However, I was really learning to live by faith. I thought I was painting a house. However, I was really learning who I truly was *in Christ.*

Unbeknownst to me at the time, God had taken me on a journey and had equipped me for battle. As a result, when Satan jabbed with his same ol' song and dance, my new mind was refusing to dance. When Satan crossed with a powerful enticement, the Spirit countered that *Christ in me* was stronger. When the Father of Lies hooked with a reminder that "I'm an addict," my shield of faith was ready and was intercepting the blow and extinguishing the lie. And finally, when the Prince of Darkness tried to sneak in a nasty uppercut reminding me, "Steinmeyer, you don't have what it takes!" the truth of the Word of God rose up within me declaring that, "Yep, I don't have what it takes, *but Jesus does, and he is within me, and he has set me free!"*

"When you know who you are, you'll know what to do!"

Now, show me – sand the floor!

16

Brian's Journey: "This Is NOT *Jurassic Park*!"

My name is Brian Ellingson, and this is my journey to freedom.

I was twelve, my brother sixteen, and we shared a room together. My brother had invited a couple of his friends over to watch a movie together. He told me unequivocally that I was not invited and kicked me out of my own room. Then, adding insult to injury, he informed me that the film they would be enjoying was the masterpiece of all masterpieces, Stephen Spielberg's *Jurassic Park*. How could I be denied a seven-hundredth screening of the greatest movie of all time? I mean real, actual, animatronic dinosaurs, bro! In true little-brother fashion, I would not be denied the opportunity to crash his party.

I opened the door the first time to barge right in, but the movie was shut off so quickly that I knew something had to be wrong. I also noticed that the VHS had been ejected from the player and switched by one of his friends. *Hmm, a mystery.*

"What are you watching?" I asked in my nosiest of nosy voices.

"Nothing dude," he countered quickly, "I already told you. It's *Jurassic Park.*" His friend held the VHS's title-side toward me as proof.

"Okay," I said, trying to sound convinced while at the same time formulating a plan to be more cunning. I walked away, fully intent on returning as silently as possible to catch my brother's dishonesty in full view. *What could he be watching that he would need to hide?* I wondered.

A short while later, I snuck down the hall slowly and quietly. And as sneakily as I could, I opened the door on a visual that would haunt me for the rest of my life. To this very day I can still feel the half-eaten, lightly toasted tuna fish sandwich that was in my hand and taste the mixture of sweet bread and tuna salad on my tongue at the moment that both my innocence was lost and that I became hooked. I still do not know who that woman was, but I knew for sure that she was not Dr. Ellie Sattler, the renowned paleobotanist, AND THIS WAS NOT *JURASSIC PARK*!

This was my first exposure to the drug of pornography.

Some would say that "drug" is a harsh word to use, and previously in my life, I would have readily agreed with them. However, there is an overwhelming amount of research showing undeniably that pornography stimulates the brain in the same way that drugs like cocaine do. No wonder it's so addictive! At twelve years old (later than many children do today, the average age being eight), I had tapped a well of instant sexual gratification and the dopamine response that accompanies it.

Interestingly, pornography is a double-edged sword. *In the moment* I felt satisfaction and pleasure. However, after the deed was done, I would recoil into darkness and self-loathing trying desperately and futilely to justify myself in an effort to push the shame away. In my mind, I would declare: "It's okay"; "It's normal"; "Everyone does it"; "I'm not as dirty as I feel right now." All the while, another voice was whispering in the depth of my psyche like the roll of distant thunder signaling a storm: "No, it's not okay, and neither are you"; "You are filthy, and you deserve to be alone"; "No one could love someone like you." I found myself trapped in a whirlwind of confusion between competing voices and between competing desires.

I wanted to feel good, and "in the moment" it *did* feel good, and numbness was more convenient than pain. And, although the feeling was fleeting (or at least it always has been in the past), I reasoned that what I was *facing right now* was worse than what I might feel afterwards. Of course, that was a lie because I invariably did feel worse. Yet every time

I would find myself thinking, *this time it's finally different; this time it's finally going to be ok.*

Of course, now in my soberness (actually, *in my realized freedom!*), I see that I was simply attempting to medicate the brokenness in my soul and mind with a Band-Aid reasoning that my drug must be good medicine because it seemed (at least briefly) to alleviate the symptoms, namely "the pain." Yet, deep down in my heart of hearts, I also knew that this medicine wouldn't cure me just like ibuprofen won't cure a broken femur.

A broken femur would seem to be a pretty obvious problem for most people. Most of us would think, "Well, duh, that needs professional medical attention." However, when it comes to wounds of our souls, they are much more subtle, and I would argue, have even more devastating and lasting effects. These wounds are often so traumatic that we cover them up, even hiding them from ourselves, because we just don't have the tools to properly deal with them. In this way we continue to medicate a disease we are unaware of except at a very minimal level. We know something is wrong that won't get better, but we also know how to deaden the pain enough to survive the day. All the while, we're stuck on a crazy cycle of shame, isolation, and lies, both to ourselves as well as others.

This was the emotional roller-coaster I found myself riding from that initial not-*Jurassic-Park* encounter, through middle school, high school, and into adulthood and marriage. It's not that I really wanted to use pornography. I didn't. However, I was stuck. I didn't know how to stop or how to say "no." If that was not enough, I struggled in other ways too: thoughts of same sex attraction, severe body dysmorphia, as well as being generally promiscuous. I wanted attention from anyone who would have me, and I didn't know why. I knew it wasn't okay, but I didn't know why that was either.

It was at this time in my life, toward the end of high school, that I began to attend a church regularly. I was in a way-too-serious relationship with a girl, and she took me to the church she had attended as a kid, and together we joined the youth group. And at that church and in that youth group I met Shawn who became a very good friend and instrumental in my own journey to faith and freedom.

Shawn led worship for that youth group, playing both the guitar and singing, and had been in this church his whole life. We started hanging out all the time and became thick as thieves. I really wanted to be like him. I had always loved music and singing but never thought I had what it took. Over the course of time, it came up that I loved music and could play guitar as well, so we began to jam out together.

Shawn persistently encouraged me, telling me that I had a really good voice, that I could play well, and that I should go public with my gift. And, though I believed he meant what he said, I could not bring myself to play in church for the youth group. Every time I would get close to my musical dream, I would bail. "I'm just too nervous," I would say; "besides, you don't really want me up there." The truth was, however, that there was another and greater reason I couldn't get past my apprehension.

Even though I had actually begun to believe in my ability as a singer and musician, I also knew my personal life was far from worthy of the call and the tug I was starting to feel in my heart. How could I perform *these* songs on *this* platform when my life was still such a mess? How could I lead people closer to Jesus when I had pushed myself so far away from him? Or had I?

It was dark and kind of chilly in the old church basement when the music started…

I see the city lights all around me
Everyone's obscure
Ten million people each with their problems
Oh, why should anyone care?
(And in Your eyes I can see)

I am not just a man vastly lost in this world
Lost in a sea of faces
Your body's the bread, Your blood is the wine
Because You traded Your life for mine [1]

The song seems a little cheesy to me now, but I'll never forget it because it was the song God broke into to speak to me. And in that moment, it was like I was the only person in the room. No one else could hear, but it was audible to me, at least the part when he called my name: "Brian."

Me? I questioned in my mind.

"Yes, Brian. I see you," he answered.

But why? Why would You even look at me?

"I see you," he asserted.

Immediately, I began to weep. God sees me! A wretch like me, someone so broken, and yet he sees me. Not just sees me, but talks to me, loves me, wants ME! Suddenly I wanted to change everything, and I was willing to give up anything for him. I didn't want this moment to end.

When the moment did finally end, there was some more music and a short sermon that I honestly can't remember, but I couldn't shake what God had just said to me. That very night, I asked the youth pastor where I should start reading my Bible, and he got me going in the right direction. I would make more changes in my life, trying to make everything *just perfect* so he wouldn't leave me now that he had come so close.

I wanted to do more, and so I drummed up the courage and asked the pastor about serving on the worship team. As I expected (and feared), he would ask me about my way-too-serious girlfriend. I knew I had to be honest (though I sure didn't want to) about us living together, and this became an impasse. I left the short meeting very disheartened. This girl was now my fiancée after all. How could I just break it off? Would she even understand?

I asked Shawn for advice, and he told me that I already knew what I needed to do. Also, that if it was God's plan for us to be together, then it would work out. This sounded pretty good to me, and that's what I told her – specifically, that we needed to go slower and resist our sexual urges with one another. She did not take this news and the new plan too well, and, truthfully, neither did I. All the while I was making all these changes in my life, I had this nagging feeling that I was missing something big about God. However, I figured that if I just kept on changing my life around, this "nagging" would work itself out eventually.

Shortly after putting the sexual brakes on in our relationship, my fiancée left me deciding she didn't feel like putting her life on hold for me. This was an enormous blow and knocked the wind fully out of my sails. I began to spiral very quickly. I got very angry with this God "who loved me so much" that he would ruin my whole life. I was questioning everything. *What am I doing wrong? Isn't this what You want? I am giving everything up and changing all of my behavior and… losing and losing. Don't you even care?* I began drinking heavily and making several other morally questionable decisions as well as leaving this church where God had spoken to me. Still, I could never quite shake that feeling from the basement. God still wanted me, even if, I pretended, I didn't want him.

A short time passed, and I met a new girl, Iris, and together we started attending a new church. I still wouldn't go on a Sunday morning because I was still too hurt. However, I went to a small group to which I was invited by a friend. It was a safe place where we could talk about what was going on in our lives: the things that were hard, the victories, and new ways God was moving. Their answers were all too familiar: "Just change your ways"; "Repent of your sin"; "Turn and go the other way." While attending this group, I realized that I was not alone in my struggles but was just one of many who did the things they knew they shouldn't and felt endless shame because of it. Also, I started admitting that pornography was "bad," and I started doing better at controlling my addiction. On the other hand, I still couldn't bring myself to confess how bad pornography was *for me* nor the depth of my addiction. I would stay guarded, in part, because I still felt shame and condemnation but also because I still didn't understand the incredible impact that pornography was having on my relationships.

It's interesting to look back over my life and to see with such clarity little moments that played such key roles in my own journey to freedom. One such moment was a phone call from my friend Shawn. Someone he knew from years before was coming to lead worship for the next few weeks (or months) while he was preparing to plant a new church in another city. That man's name is Mel. Shawn encouraged me to talk with Mel, saying that he was a good man who might be able to help me become a worship leader (still a dream I carried). However, I was still cautious, so I just stuck my toe in the water.

When Mel finally arrived, I found myself going to the worship practices and just hanging around. However, one day I dared to share with him my dream of being on *that stage* and leading worship to and for Jesus. "Why aren't you?" he asked. *Uh oh! Here we go again.*

Again, I told the truth, "Because I'm living with my girlfriend [Iris], and my life isn't really perfect."

"Jesus meets you were you're at," Mel countered.

Mel had not only upended my objection but my whole understanding of God and his love for me. Hope filled my heart as I fought back the tears. It was just like my encounter in the basement. Jesus had never left me. God was never far off. I had been hiding, but he had never lost sight of me. Jesus meets me where I am. I don't have to dress up to come to him, because he dressed down, became a man, and came to me.

I began to play bass with the team at practices, and, though I struggled with stage fright, I would begin playing more and more. When Mel left to go plant his new church, I left too. However, I didn't leave God this time and continued to attend other local churches with Iris and with a renewed sense of God's presence. He loves me even when I'm dirty, even when I'm not doing everything right. Also,

Iris and I eventually got married. We quit making excuses and admitted that we couldn't keep playing house when God was calling us to be and do so much more. Our own half-hearted lifestyle was hurting our chances of helping others get closer to him. Once we were married, a huge weight lifted from both of us and we were able to go to church without feeling judged or condemned by our own consciences.

A year and a half later, I got another call from Shawn, this time informing me that Mel was heading back to the Tri-Cities where he was becoming the new senior pastor of his church because his current pastor was retiring. I couldn't wait to go back and help the man who had helped me so much by sharing one of the greatest revelations I had ever received. As a side note, Mel couldn't remember saying that to me but admitted it was both pretty good and absolutely true. As Mel stepped into the leadership role, Iris and I began to serve as well. Iris served in the nursery while I served on the worship team, and we served pretty much everywhere else we could as well. Mel began to train me as a worship leader for our church (Gateway Church in Kennewick, WA), which is where I still serve today. In fact, Mel mentored me and helped me to become a pastor myself. More than that, Mel became my friend who God would use to help me walk in true freedom. However, freedom didn't come in a single day; it was a journey.

I had gotten to a point where I could control my urges most of the time. I assumed that's just how life was going to be forever, and besides, as long as I kept it to myself, I wasn't hurting anyone but myself anyway, right? **Wrong! Wrong! Wrong**! What a ridiculous lie. The truth I would discover was that my indulgences were deeply wounding my wife, in addition to deepening the wounds in my own heart. By God's incredible mercy, I got caught.

Somehow, I had left something open on my phone, and as Iris saw it, I could see the searing pain in her heart as she discovered I had eyes for someone else. I have never physically cheated on my wife. However, in the moment she beheld the object to which my gaze had fallen instead of her, her heart was shattered. I knew this was the end. All my worst fears were about to be realized as she came to know the real me, the dirty, disgusting creature she had married – not a human man, but a worthless pile of refuse. How could she ever forgive me? How could we ever recover from this? "I'm so sorry, can you forgive me?" I said, bawling.

"It's ok," she said through tears of her own, "I forgive you. I still love you."

We sat crying together as I admitted that I didn't have nearly the control I thought or pretended, I did. She asked me if I would talk to pastor Mel, and I told her I would. Pastor Mel had already helped me find real faith and hope by helping me change my thinking (true repentance!) about God and his love for me. Could he also help me to find true freedom as well? Both Iris and I were really hoping so. On the other hand, had Pastor Mel even found true freedom for himself yet? He had been honest with our congregation that he had struggled with pornography. Was he still struggling? I was about to discover the answers to these questions as my own incredible journey to freedom would begin finally moving in the right direction. And one of those first steps on that journey was this moment of experiencing the indescribable grace and mercy of Jesus through my wife, Iris.

Mel and I began to have a lot of conversations. He recommended some books I should read on this issue. Most importantly, we became accountability partners so that we could call on each other whenever we were struggling (i.e., failing). And because we were (and still are) really good friends, being accountable to one another was both safe and encouraging rather than something to fear. As a result, we both got much better at controlling our lustful temptations as we kept an open line of communication and extended grace to one another. And yet a truth (the kind that sets you free) still eluded us.

Sure, we were not messing up as often, and we were better at bouncing our gaze. Yet we remained trapped in a constant battle between our own strength and the overwhelming inadequacy of our own ability to save ourselves from *anything.* But this is the way it is, right? Every man must *battle* all the days of his life if he wants to be free. And while it was true that Mel and I both seemed to be *better* at battling, war didn't *feel* very much like freedom to either of us. There seems a grievous disparity here.

One day, while reading *Pure Desire* by Ted Roberts[2] (one of the books Mel had recommended that I read) a truth about the interconnectedness between childhood trauma and the lingering effects that result in triggers that drive many into porn (and other substances) as an attempt to medicate those deep wounds, intrigued me. I had never thought of it like that, and it made perfect sense. As a result, I was challenged to take a deep inward look at my own life to see what could have caused me to end up here. As I did so, so many things became clear.

For so much of my life, I have had such a debilitating sense of worthlessness. Where did this come from? As I pondered that question, a memory crystallized in my mind about who I believed I was. As a young teen while I was performing a chore at our house, one of my parents entered the scene. They were drunk and declared rhetorically, "Why don't you go live somewhere else so things will get done right around here?" Although I had forgotten that memory, I had never forgotten that feeling. The mining of my past revealed other moments like this that were long buried in the back of my mind. It was the wound that wouldn't heal: "You'll never be enough, and no one will ever love you enough to stay because you're just not worth it."

In an instant, so many things made so much sense: my incredible sense of insecurity with my wife, my job, my calling into ministry, my kids; my need to control everything; and my constant struggle to feel good. This is who I was because this had been my name for as long as I could remember. However, God began to show me something altogether different: the possibility of a new name and a new identity.

At the same time, I had also been struggling with spinal arthritis. We were at a youth event (Iris and I were now youth leaders at Gateway) where God would touch my back *and more.* The speaker was both charismatic and encouraging, and many of the youth there would respond to the altar call. I was among them, both to support the members of our own youth group who were yielding their lives to God but also because I wanted God to heal *me.* While at the altar, God would once again speak to me in that still small voice, "Brian, I can heal your back, but I really want to heal your heart." And, once again, the tears began to flow. How could I resist his love for me? I surrendered, and that night God healed both my back and my heart. Of course, the heart is a trickier thing to heal, and the process is still ongoing. As for my back, it was healed completely and has been now for many years. In fact, recently I ran a half marathon, something I could not possibly do before.

As I look back on my past, and my own journey that God has taken me on, it's so interesting (and wonderful!) to see how God was preparing me to realize my own freedom almost simultaneously with Mel. As Mel's accountability partner, friend, and associate pastor I would share candidly about what I was reading as well as things God was showing me, and Mel would share the same things with me. As a result, my front row seat to God's deliverance of Mel contributed to my own deliverance as well.

When Pastor Mel was reading *Feels Like Redemption*[3] and couldn't shake that thought that "freedom oughta' feel free," I was one of the ones he shared this with first, as well as when Jesus spoke to him about how he was *already* free but just hadn't realized it yet. I was there in that first *Faith Discovery* class, where he shared our baseball-diamond model for what it means to be a disciple of Jesus and that faith is first base and when he had his Holy-Spirit-inspired-epiphany moment. I was there when he asked us, "What do we say when we mess up?" And I heard it with my own ears when someone responded, "I promise I'll *do* better." And when he asked us, "How many of us say something like that when we mess up?", I too raised my hand. And I was there when he showed us how this was running to third base to somehow get God's approval, of which we already had, how we needed to run to first base and believe that God *already* loves us perfectly and has *already* set us free, and how the Holy Spirit within us gives the power to both love and obey.

At this same time, and on my own journey, I was working my way through Paul's letter to the Ephesians, specifically studying chapter six and the armor of God. In verse seventeen of that chapter Paul exhorts us to…

...take the helmet of salvation and the sword of the Spirit, which is the word of God.

As Mel unpacks in chapter twelve, the word Paul uses here and that we translate "word," is the Greek word *rhema,* which means the literal spoken words of God. With this understanding as my foundation, Mel comes to me like a kid who just won a free trip to Disney World (maybe more excited) and tells me what Jesus has spoken to him the night before about him being already free and how he remembers at that very moment John 8:36,*"So if the Son sets you free, you will be free indeed."* And right away, I recognized that this is *rhema*. In fact, these are the very words spoken by Jesus. This is the sword of the Spirit that causes the enemy to flee. *Whom the Son sets free is free indeed!* This is the truth of who we are: *we are free indeed!*

To the one on the outside looking in, finding freedom may seem like it comes like flipping a switch when suddenly the world changes from dark to light. However, that is not the reality. Without all the little moments – God meeting me in the basement of the church, Mel helping me see that Jesus meets us right where we are, the healing of my back and my heart, the revealing of and the healing of my wounds – I may never have been able to *believe* what Mel had discovered, nor would I have seen its connection to what God was already showing me in Ephesians. I too was on a journey to freedom. All along, God was building my faith in the background, not because he needed to but because *I needed him* to. And because he is a good Father, he was patient, merciful, gracious, and loving toward me through it all.

Before my journey to freedom, I probably would have laughed when Mel told me that he had simply spoken to his temptation and the enemy that he was free. However, God had prepared me to believe. And since that time, I too have effectively wielded that same weapon against lust and pornography: *I am free because Jesus says I'm free.* I know now who I am and *whose* I am. As a result, like Mel, I too have been walking in freedom for almost seven years now. That doesn't mean I'm not tempted anymore or that I'm perfect, and I certainly haven't "arrived."

As I was preparing to write out my testimony for this book, I came under a vicious attack. In a moment when I was alone and isolated from the people who love me, the enemy began to whisper those old familiar lies: "You're not who you pretend to be"; "Everyone is going to find out that you're a failure and your testimony won't help anyone"; "Why bother? You'll just hurt more people." As I sat in the deafening silence of my office, I fought what seemed to be a losing battle with my own thoughts, even giving into the temptation, and all the while feeling like the fraud the accuser was saying I was.

Spiritual maturity, however, is not perfection but getting back up more quickly when you fall. So, I called my wife, Iris, thinking that if I could just tell her I was struggling, that would help. And it did help, but the temptation would not go away. In my heart of hearts, I knew I needed to call Mel. However, at the same time, I didn't want him to know that I was in trouble – not after all we had fought for. How could I admit my failure without damaging our whole ministry?

After three tortuous days, I finally called Mel. I fully expected him to reprimand me sternly and to scold me. However, once again, I was surprised by grace. Mel simply asked, "Why didn't you call me earlier?" And then he reminded me of the truth and called me back towards faith. "You're still free" he declared, "A stumble doesn't change who you are. You're okay. I love you, man." A stumble can never rob us of our identity as children of God, nor does it diminish the power of his Holy Spirit living in us and making us truly and completely free.

No matter your struggle, whether it's pornography or whatever, if you have put your trust in Jesus, then you are a child of God. He gave ALL who believe in him that right.[4] I challenge you to look back over your life and see the work of God's hand in it even, I believe, to leading you to this book. Now *believe* and declare your freedom today and every day because, if the Son has set you free, *you are free indeed!*

17

Jon's Journey: Life from Ashes

I found myself once again in the pit of despair and blackness created by my unfaithfulness. Only this time I felt there was no hope for me, and I turned my heart away from God and my wife. I could not confess again. I could not admit again, after all these years, after all the confessions and after all the forgiveness I had already received. I could not face my wife again. I knew that if I spilled my guts and she knew what I had done, she would leave me. I gave up on any hope of restoration and turned inward into emptiness. Everything was burned over; there was nothing left.

However, Julie knew something was wrong and would not let it go. There were many nights of tears where she begged me to open up to her, but I would not. Then one night, after many months of this, I said to myself, *"Why not tell her? It doesn't matter. It's over. She's going to leave you anyway,"* and I confessed everything to her. There were events from the past that I had kept secret from her that had to be uncovered as well. It was a long, hard night. Julie was nonemotional as I confirmed what she had already sensed in her heart. I had confessed but was unrepentant.

Then a miracle happened…

My name is Jon Carter. I have known Mel since we attended Northwest University together in Kirkland, WA in the 1980s. It was also at Northwest where I met Mel's sister, Julie. We fell in love and were married shortly after I graduated. I would love to tell you that we lived happily ever after. However, I was tremendously wounded, and this manifested itself in both our dating and for many years into our marriage. This is our story and my journey to freedom.

I really like the way Dr. Dan Allender emphasizes how valuable and therapeutic it is to share our journeys (which he calls "our stories") with others. More importantly, however, is our desperation for others to hear us, believe us, and validate us.[1] Still, a more amazing revelation in our journeys is how God in his grace is continually intersecting with them until we finally surrender our demand to be in charge, allowing him to redeem and heal us and forever changing their trajectory. My theology professor at Northwest, Dr. Dan Pecota, used to always remind us, "It is God who initiates, and we can only respond."

Because of this fact, our story (Julie and I as a couple) is mostly about my story (my addiction) and how God unrelentingly and lovingly initiated grace into our lives and the tragedy and triumph of our responses to him. On the other hand, it is "our story" because it is about my wife as much as it is about me: my struggles with a sexual-medication lifestyle and God's grace, mercy, forgiveness, and love being repeatedly poured out through Julie, my wife. She – in her typical insightful way – has said, "When God made Jon, he knew he was going to have a very hard time of it, and so he asked himself, 'What gift can I give my son to help him through it?' and so he gave me to you." This has been so true. There have been many times that I have said, "I don't know where I would be if it had not been for my wife allowing the grace of God to work through her." I'm pretty sure I would be rolled up in a ditch somewhere.

My story is one of a very serious, devout Christian kid/young man/adult who always wanted to serve God, live a "good Christian life," and who dreamed of "changing the world for Jesus"...*if only I could get rid of a "small little problem" with sexual misbehavior.* I dedicated my life to Christ, went forward for an altar call, and was baptized at the age of seven. I attended a Christian school and a Spirit-filled church and received the baptism in the Holy Spirit at the age of thirteen. I wanted to be a missionary, went on several mission trips, led people to Christ, and eventually went to Bible College (i.e., Northwest) and entered the ministry as a pastor. However, underneath it all was a wounded heart, a distorted view of God, and a secret method of medicating the wound that doomed that life-path to failure, disgrace, and shame.

A young man asked me the other day, "I understand the addiction and I understand the wound, but how did the two get connected?" A great question! I believe that we are all wounded in one way or another and usually when we are young. Until we were hurt so grievously, we were okay, and we *felt* okay. Now we feel anything *but* okay and just want to be validated in some way. Some of us receive this validation through a healthy family or another healing relationship. However, for many of us that's not our world. This is why we're so susceptible to that *FREE* (and usually *secret*) sample of "medicine" (e.g., pornography, an extramarital affair, workaholism, alcoholism or some other substance abuse, etc.) that Satan, our friendly neighborhood pusher, offers us. This "medicine" promises to give us the validation we seek or, at the bare minimum, at least take the edge off the pain we're in. Except it's not really medicine but a trap that will ensnare our body, mind, and soul. We don't *mean* to get addicted. We're simply attempting to medicate our pain. Of course, when we finally sober up, we realize that we now have two problems: the original wound that is still hemorrhaging and now an addiction to something that is not only incapable of healing us, but is, in fact, making our lives much worse.

This too is my story. *My wound* was infused with a message that said: "You are unworthy," "You're not good enough," "No one really wants you," "You are not enough." Those messages, combined with a distorted view, which believed that God only really loved me because he had to (after all, I was part of the "whole world" he said he loved so much), poisoned my identity. I did not know who I was or "whose" I was and was searching for something to validate my masculine identity. I believed I was pretty much on my own, needing to find God, draw him out, make him notice me, and somehow convince him to like me. If he was choosing up teams, I was certain he would only select me because I was the last one left. I sometimes wonder if I had reasoned that entering pastoral ministry was my ultimate career enhancement because *then* he would have to like me, seeing all my good effort.

Early in my life, I was convinced sex and sexual behavior (even kissing) was bad, and even *wanting it* was bad. It was something guys always wanted but girls (not wanting it) gave grudgingly to get what they really wanted. The terrible twin epiphanies came in college when I discovered that some girls *like* being sexual, and, *worse,* I felt powerful and desired when they would interact with me in this way. And there you have it: my wound's life-long search for its medication was over, resulting in an addiction that took on a life of its own. Though somehow stopping short of intercourse, I used girls to alleviate my loneliness, medicate my pain, and provide me an identity. Even though I was a nobody on campus, somehow I felt more virulent and remarkable having made out with some girl the night before, even though I was the only one who knew.

Like so many, I thought marriage would solve everything. It didn't. In fact, it was driven deeper underground into even more secret, powerful, shameful, and destructive pathways. We must have our drug! The reality after marriage for me was that, in a very sinister way, the desire to be involved with other women took on an even *more* powerful attraction and disabling entitlement. It was more powerful because there were more moral lines to cross and more entitled because I could blame it on my wife that she wasn't meeting my needs.

Julie also discovered that the behavior I modeled with her prior to marriage while we were dating wasn't satiated after our marriage. This led me to several tearful, well-intended confessions after repeated, ever-deepening occasions of unfaithfulness. Each round of acting out, getting caught, and confessing grew more physical until I engaged in a full sexual affair that went on for months. Eventually, the secret became public, requiring the official ministerial discipline, revocation of my license and ordination, and the loss of our ministry. My life and our marriage were in total destruction and free-fall. My Band-Aid was a week at a life-recovery clinic in California, spending time with several counselors and a decision to move away from the area of my temptation, to put some distance between me and my tempters, and to start anew elsewhere. We chose Idaho.

After our relocation from Washington to Idaho, I would go long stretches without acting out. This was not due to my ability to live in victory, but, instead, totally due to the mercy and intervention of God who, I believe, thwarted any of my attempts to find willing partners. It was during this time that pornography stepped in to fill the gap. Long weeks traveling for work and boring hours waiting in the airport helped cultivate this new avenue of medication. There were also years of *feeling* victorious and living a fairly sober life, during which times we were volunteers in ministry at our church and even tried to help other couples with their marriages. However, I was not, by any means, free.

The Scripture says that after Satan left Jesus from tempting him in the wilderness, "He left him until an opportune time."[3] As much as God is patient and unrelenting in his love for us, our enemy is unrelenting in his hatred for us, waiting for that "opportune time" to reopen the unhealed wounds and spread his poison in our hearts again. It is at that moment we once again reach for the medication offered us. And reach I did; after all, addiction is a kind of slavery that will not let you say, "no," especially when you are feeling alone and hurting. And, once again, as I mentioned at the beginning of this chapter, I found myself in that pit of despair and blackness created by my unfaithfulness. Except this time, there was no plan, no scheme, and no hope. I had come to the end of myself and decided to confess to Julie *everything* and braced myself for the abandonment I knew that was coming and that I absolutely deserved. And then that miracle happened...

Julie did not leave me...*but loved me.* The enemy had convinced me that if she knew the truth about me, she would see me for the monster I knew I was, would despise me the way I despised myself, and would crush me, sending me away. I would be empty and alone, like a burned-over forest after a terrible fire. However, God initiated, and I responded by opening up to Julie. I saw the love of God *for me* for the first time in my life in the eyes of my wife. She knew all and still loved me. I saw the forgiveness of God *for me* and *my life* in the arms of my wife.

A few days after the original confession, and in response to Julie's grace for me, I moved past mere words, humbling myself and, with a truly broken and contrite heart, asked her to forgive me. And my view of the entire world changed. In a very dramatic way, all that had been gray and dismal became alive and full of color. The sky was bluer, the hills greener, and I was alive again. It is hard to describe the actual change that occurs in the physical when the spiritual is resurrected, but it is real and dramatic. You don't know just how dark your heart has become until you step back into the light, and my heart had been very dark and dead. However, *NOW*, where there had only been burned-over ashes of what had been my life, there sprouted a green stem of God's resurrection-goodness and new life...what I like to call *regeneration life.* Where we see only death and destruction, God in his goodness and mercy brings new life, a little green sprout of hope. There are no hopeless situations in God's economy. There are no lives that are so messed up that he can't make something beautiful of them.

Since then, I have been on a journey of rediscovering God, not made in my own distorted image, but for who he really is – the Lover of my soul. I love the line from the movie *The Shack* when Papa (God) admits that he is extremely fond of all of us.[4] *God is extremely fond of me.* What a wonderful discovery! When I finally understood how much he truly loves me *and is fond of me,* I was led to my true identity as a son of God. As was quoted earlier, "When you know who you are, you know what to do," but I cannot know who I am without understanding I am the personal object of my loving Father's deep affection. What others say about me and how they treat me do not dictate who I am. When my identity is secure in him, then I am on a solid footing that allows me to choose to respond in grace and goodness to the world around me instead of victimizing others to medicate my wounded, broken heart. God is all about healing hearts.

I am also on a journey of allowing God to take me back into my wounds and to heal me, setting me free. When we are just trying to modify our behavior, we settle for short term solutions, asking God to give us a Band-Aid or make the pain stop. We try to "white knuckle" our way into a new behavior. I am no longer having to "white knuckle" my way through life. For when we allow Jesus into our woundedness and allow him to heal us, we no longer have to medicate, compensate, or hide. We can be free, *"Free Indeed!"* I see so much more clearly now what Jesus had been inviting me into all along but I had been refusing. I had wanted God to build me a stronger cage, *but he wanted to set me free!*

None of us make it through this life without being wounded by something or someone. These wounds are delivered with a message about us, God, and the world around us (like Mel shared in chapter fifteen and that John Eldridge calls the "message of the arrows"[5]). However, healing comes through a prayerful process of allowing Jesus into those tender, wounded, and broken places of our heart and where we allow him to speak a new message of truth and hope.

Now, on the other side of freedom and healing, when I feel my heart react in pain or disappointment and I feel the desire to hide or medicate, I can ask my heart, "What am I feeling, and what lie am I believing about myself, my world, or my God?" Then I can allow my loving Father what truth he wants to show me to draw me into deeper and more complete healing. And because God is neither surprised nor ever ashamed of me, every moment of acting out or being tempted to act out can be an invitation to enter healing.[6]

One of the keys when your heart is at this point is to listen to your Father in heaven and allow him to take your heart on a journey. What am I feeling? Why am I feeling this? When did I first feel this? What messages are attached to this? In what way am I using my unwanted behavior to compensate, medicate, or hide this feeling and message? How does Jesus want to bring healing to this? This may seem complicated, but every temptation or activity is an invitation into healing. As my friend Greg Wingard used to say, "Every temptation is the enemy trying to strike you out, but it is still a pitch over the plate and is also your opportunity to hit a home run." Our Father God is a loving expert coach helping us and empowering us to hit a home run. Let's make it a grand slam! In fact, if you've put your trust in Jesus, he has *already* equipped you to hit with *his power*:

> *...for it is God who works in you to will and to act in order to fulfill his good purpose.*[7]

18

Chase's Journey: "One Thing I Do Know"

I was thirteen years old, and it was my first crush. And as much as any thirteen-year-old could be, I was head over heels in love. At that point in my life, I had absolutely no fear in my heart and was quite brave but, then again, I hadn't been hurt yet. I was so confident that Stacy (not her real name) would say "yes!" to me, and it was all I was expecting to hear. Unfortunately, I had shared my fondness for this girl with the wrong people, and news got out that I liked her...*which Stacy discovered as well.* I still wasn't afraid though. In fact, it stiffened my resolve. I would not be deterred! Come hell or high water, I was going to ask Stacy to "go with me." So, that's exactly what my confident, brave thirteen-year-old self did. I asked her. Unfortunately, my little thirteen-year-old heart was not prepared for what would happen next.

One of the things I discovered was that when your buddies say, "The worst thing that could happen is that she could say "No" is an absolute lie! Let me explain. The moment of truth had arrived, but when I meandered up to Stacy in the hallway and opened my mouth to demonstrate what a silver-tongued Casanova I was, the unthinkable happened. Before I could even finish a single sentence, Stacy burst into laughter...*and the surrounding crowd laughed as well.* I didn't get a "no"; I got made fun of. I was devastated and confused. It was the first time my heart would be pierced by rejection. And if that was not enough, it was going to get worse.

Whether this was due to denial or naivety, I'm not sure, but what I reasoned in my head was that Stacy didn't *actually* reject me because I had never finished asking her out. In fact, she had cut me off midsentence keeping me from doing so. Man, was I an idiot! The next day, I tried again, and lightning struck twice. The very same thing happened *again!* And I don't just mean *kind of*, or *like*, or *sort of*. Once again, before I could even finish my sentence, asking Stacy to be my girlfriend, she cut me off midsentence and erupted into laughter. And, *again, everyone* laughed with her. I'm sure you can imagine how embarrassed and rejected I felt. How was I ever going to live this down? A simple "no" would have been nice but, instead, my young and impressionable heart was impaled with a wound that is still not fully healed.

My name is Chase Steinmeyer, and Mel is my dad. As I am writing this, I am twenty-two years old and a senior at Life Pacific, a Christian university in San Dimas, California. I am studying to become a Senior Pastor like my father before me. In fact, I will be a third-generation pastor, as my grandfather (my mom's dad) also went to Life Pacific (then called "Life Bible College") and was a pastor for well over forty years before retiring from vocational ministry in 2012. My goal and passion is to help people understand who God is, how great of a Father he is, and what a wonderful privilege it is to be invited to participate in his mission, helping even more people become his children. I am also single. This is my journey from woundedness, to being a slave to pornography, to realizing my freedom, and to walking in that freedom as a single man.

To be honest, I would rather be married and sharing my life with that special someone. In fact, when I was struggling so tremendously, it so frustrated me to hear from my dad and Brian *how easy it was* to walk in freedom, yet they both had someone to go to when they felt alone or tempted. I, on the other hand, didn't just feel alone, *I was alone*...and I used this at times as an excuse for giving in to sin. Maybe that's how you feel. Maybe that's your reality too. Don't despair. It is not impossible for you to walk in freedom as a single person. In fact, I am living proof that the power of the Gospel works for everyone, including us single people. I too can say now, *it's pretty easy*. My hope in sharing my story is that you will discover this same reality for yourself.

As I have already shared, my story begins with a wound, and a very painful one at that.

> *"Are you in pain, Frodo?" said Gandalf quietly as he rode by Frodo's side.*
>
> *"Well, yes I am," said Frodo. "It is my shoulder. The wound aches, and the memory of darkness is heavy on me. It was a year ago today."*
>
> *"Alas! there are some wounds that cannot be wholly cured," said Gandalf.*[1]

Time may pass, but the wound may keep on aching. I agree with Gandalf that some wounds may never wholly be cured until we meet with Christ face to face. If I am being honest, my wound still aches at the thought of it. However, I would be a liar if I said Jesus has done no healing at all for it; alas, this healing is a journey that he is still taking me on.

I do not wish what happened to me on anybody. I have struggled with rejection to this day because of it. And while that one event didn't push me into pornography, *it sure kept me in it!* After being rejected, my confidence was shot. Instead of being brave, I was now afraid. In fact, I now felt worthless – my wound ever declaring to me that I was less than enough. I had confidence in other things, thankfully, but that too would also be undermined.

I worked so hard to prove my worth through high

school football. Yet it was not to be. Whether I was not good enough or noticeable enough, either way I was left feeling worthless in that area as well. I so desperately wanted to be the *best* at something because then it would *prove* that I was good enough. However, I found I was never good enough in anything I tried. As a result, this single event that wounded me so grievously also set me on a course that was an impossible mission…*to be good enough.* This was not something I wanted for myself or cared about. I just wanted *others* to think I was good enough. This driving and unrelenting force both led to pornography and left me stuck in it. Growing up, no one had made me feel good enough. On the contrary, a lot of people had rejected me – even close friends. Through pornography, however, I discovered *someone* who would not reject me. It was only fantasy, though, so, instead of making me feel better, it made everything worse. Pornography couldn't fix my situation. In fact, it was another knife deepening the wound.

Larger and deeper my wound would become, affecting and *infecting* everything I did, especially my thinking. It seemed that everything I would do, my mind would correlate with being rejected by a woman. If I was not good at playing guitar, surely I would get rejected. If I was bad at football, what woman would want me? If I didn't know the Bible, what *Christian woman* would want me? All my failures were pushing me towards these beautiful two-dimensional women who *couldn't* reject me. At the same time, this secret life was also making me even more miserable. This was not the abundant life Jesus promised me,[2] and I needed to *try harder* to obtain that.

It was hard to admit my addiction to someone else and to submit myself to being accountable to them, but I gutted it up and did just that. And I did the other things you're supposed to do to get free as well. For five years, I *tried harder*, and it was complete insanity; doing the same things and expecting different results. Nothing changed…*until* the Holy Spirit would reveal some deep truths to me.

In many of the Christian circles I find myself in, there is a popular idea at large. When addressing the issue of pornography, I've heard so many pastors preaching to *Christians* who are struggling in this area say, "You need to get free from pornography!" However, is what they are saying truly biblical and right? Is freedom a *destination* that believers need somehow to get to? Is freedom and holiness the time in between our sins? Or could it be something we've already been given and that we already have even if we haven't *experienced* it yet?

In my own journey, I've discovered that many Christians attack pornography like *the world* attacks pornography (at least the part of the world that admits that pornography is destructive). In fact, if you compare what many churches teach about *battling* pornography to what unbelievers teach, you'll see almost no difference. Why do we do this? Why do we play the world's game and especially when it's obvious that the world's way is not a winning way? Thankfully, though, there are exceptions.

A couple of years ago, I heard a short blurb from a message by John Piper about lust and pornography that ended up being a catalyst for totally changing my thinking on self-control and freedom. In that sermon, Piper stated that we are not controlled by lust but *"by what we believe."*[3] When I heard this, the wheels began to turn in my brain. It was like the fresh air of the Holy Spirit was waking me up to what true freedom really is. And I wondered if the true follower of Jesus (indwelt by the Spirit of God) could even really be in bondage. Whereas so many were demanding that I *become* free, I began to see that Scripture was showing me that I *already was*. Whereas before I was viewing freedom as a destination. Now I was seeing that *Jesus was the destination* we should be striving for, and that freedom is wrapped up in the package when we find him. In other words, when I found Jesus and put my faith in him, I became free!

As Christians, we have a tendency to monitor our freedom in terms of timespan. If we fail, then our freedom is reset, and we must start over. Of course, this makes sense in light of our obvious circumstances. How can I be free when I just messed up, right? This is why we are so comfortable with believing this way, and I was no exception. On the other hand, this is completely the opposite of what the Bible teaches about both freedom as well as living by faith and not by sight.[4] In so many churches, we teach that we should live by faith and not by works (and we should teach this), yet at the same we also preach that we must *try harder* to become free, and if we mess up, we must *try even harder* so we can become free again. Boy, that sure sounds like living by works to me. Worse, it *feels* like living by works. Can you relate?

On the other hand, according to the Word of God, when we are saved, we become free *at that moment* and with the chains of addiction being broken forever as well. Why? Because when you believe in Jesus you are baptized into his death so that *"we too may have a new life."* Furthermore, because of your faith in Jesus, your *old self* has died, and *"...anyone who has died has been set free from sin."*[5]

So, what is freedom exactly? How can we even know what freedom feels like if we don't even know what it is? For the convict, they might feel free when they finally get to walk out of their prison cell. For the addict, they might feel free when they no longer feel the pull of their particular addictive substance. What would make *you* feel free? Thankfully, true freedom doesn't start with our feelings but with aligning ourselves with the truth and connecting it with faith. Again, as my dad already shared throughout this book, this is true repentance. Our thinking changes first as we align ourselves with God's truth, which in turn becomes our own personal reality, and feelings (like joy, peace, and freedom) follow that.

Consequently, the addict will never become free as long as they continue to think like an addict and continue to use. In other words, they will remain a slave, *which is the opposite of freedom.* This is how the Apostle Paul shows us what freedom looks like in Romans (especially chapter seven) by contrasting it with slavery. So, what is slavery? It is a life without choice. Before and without Jesus, sin is our master. We don't sin because we choose to. We sin because we are unable to choose not to. Sin is our master, and we must obey him. Freedom, on the other hand, is release from that old master and our old lifestyle. So, instead of having no choice, we have choice. Freedom is choice! Yes, we can still sin if we choose to. However, we've been set free by Jesus and are no longer under the law but under grace.[6] Furthermore, God has given us his power through his Spirit so we can choose rightly.[7] This might sound weird, but when you sin as a believer, you are *freely* sinning. Before, whether you liked it or not, you sinned. However, now Christ has given you the ability to choose.

Furthermore, this divine freedom that is gifted to those of us in Christ is not reversed by any sin we may commit. On the contrary, this freedom is solid and unwavering. After all, Christ did not take just *some* of the sin in our lives, he took it **ALL** and did away with it, thus solidifying our freedom in him.

These were the truths that the Holy Spirit was unveiling to me. Unfortunately, I was having difficulty connecting these truths to faith and my own reality. In other words, even after discovering all this about the freedom that God had given me in Christ, I still believed I was a slave to pornography. The guilt and shame of messing up made me feel this way. I looked at my life through my own eyes, and what I saw was someone who was still a slave.

I had heard my dad share over and over about that night Jesus spoke to him, "Mel, you're already free. You just haven't realized it yet." However, I had had no such experience like that. Why wouldn't Jesus speak personally to me like he did with Dad? Maybe if he did that with me, I could finally and truly believe and could then walk in freedom like Dad was doing. Then one night, the Holy Spirit inclined me to read John 8:36 for myself: *"So if the Son sets you free, you will be free indeed."* And as I did, I felt the Holy Spirit begin to move in both my heart and mind, and I began to question my own thoughts and beliefs. *I say that I am not free,* ***but Jesus says I am free.*** This led me to a profound realization: either I am the liar, or Jesus is the liar, and I know Jesus does not lie. You might be thinking "Well, duh!" However, isn't this the way so many of us live, like Jesus is the liar and that we are right?

If *you* define your identity, you will live by that identity. However, if you let *Christ* define your identity, you will live by that identity instead. You have to believe it, though. Like we rest in a chair believing it will hold our weight, we need to rest our weight upon the truth of who Jesus says we are. Jesus was speaking to me. Maybe not like he did with my dad. But he was speaking to me all the same. These were his red-letter words in John 8:36, and they were to me as much as they were to his disciples and as they are to *you* as well! That night, I began to truly believe and to take Jesus at his Word. He said I was free, and he does not lie! He had made me free, but it was *my* choice as to what I would do with that freedom.

It's your choice too. I can't realize your freedom for you. Your circumstances do not define your freedom. Other people do not define your freedom. Your past, present, and future sins do not define your freedom. Only Jesus defines your freedom! He says you're free. Don't take my word for it. *Take his.* He does not lie! Even if you sin right now, you are still free. If you get on a hot streak and go the next twenty years without sinning and then you blow out, you are still free. You're free because Jesus says so and because he said, *"It is finished."*[8] If you've put your trust in Jesus, you have *already* been redeemed and saved. It wouldn't be that much of a redemption if it was so easily undone by one sin – or a thousand for that matter.

I believe that the most pivotal part of living free is rooted in knowing who we are in Christ. According to God's Word, you are free, a child of God, a holy one, and the righteousness of God[9] whether you feel like that right now or not. God wants us to know who we are and who he has made us to be. We, however, are left with the choice as to whether or not we will believe him and take him at his Word. What will *you* choose?

One of the things I'd like to emphasize in my journey is realizing my freedom as a single man. Being single was a huge obstacle for me, and for quite some time I allowed this fact to keep me from living free in Christ. I was lonely and aching for that special someone, a best friend *in the flesh*, to satisfy that longing and to make me complete. Through many tearful and lonely nights, I would envision someone who could heal my heart so I would not have to sin anymore. To be honest, I still long for that kind of *human* relationship and interaction.

Maybe you find yourself in that same boat, thinking that marriage will fix your problem with lust and/or pornography. This is such a terrible lie the enemy uses against us. Remember, *we are controlled by what we believe.* The fact is that many (if not most) men still struggle even after they tie the knot. I think it's sad that we could be so convinced that the presence of another *mere human* could really cure what ails us. The reality is that the relationship that we think and hope would be our remedy would actually also be infected by our sin. As a result, our sin would now not only be hurting *us* but the person we love the most. Do we really want to bring that kind of pain upon someone else? I sure don't.

Along the way, God dismantled that lie in my mind, and I am I praying that he does the same in you – for your sake, for the person you will someday marry, and for your children. There is no secret formula or tip that I could give you that is geared just for us single people. The Gospel is "one size fits all." God offers the same *freedom to everyone,* and the same *strength to everyone.* That freedom (the kind that "feels free") is found in Christ alone. And that strength is the very strength of God within those of us who believe. Again, remember, it's *what we believe* that controls us.

With that said, the single most important factor that helped me realize my freedom in Christ was realizing that so much of what I believed about myself was a lie. In other words, understanding and believing who I truly am in Christ and to my Father in heaven set me free. I don't believe I am a special case or an exception. This can be your reality as well, which starts with refusing to believe the lie that you can't be free as a single person. You can! In fact, Jesus says you are *already* free. My life is a testimony (and I'm not the only one by far) that single people can live as *free* people. Take Jesus at his word and choose to live in the transformation that he brings.

I just love seeing God transform people. In fact, one of my favorite *truth* statements in the Bible is from a blind man whom Jesus healed: *"Whether he* [Jesus] *is a sinner or not, I don't know.* ***One thing I do know.*** *I was blind, but now I see!"*[10] Indeed, *one thing I do know,* I was a slave to sin, but now I'm free. Are you ready to *know* this for yourself? Then stop trusting yourself and your circumstances and begin believing Jesus.

19

Keep Steppin'

My little sister, Julie, whom you've already read a little about, also used to also play the little round ball in the spring. Although, in her case, that ball was a little larger than the one I knocked around. Julie played Little League softball. And she was pretty good at it too. Most often, she pitched and played catcher, although she could honestly play anywhere around the diamond or in the outfield. She was a very good fielder and could throw better than many of the boys I played with and against. Therefore, it wasn't surprising when she was selected for the all-star team.

Julie's one downfall was a bad habit she developed in her swing when she was batting. In fact, it was a regular occurrence to hear her coaches yell out to her when she was at the plate, "Be careful not to drop your shoulder." This morphed into, "STOP DROPPING YOUR SHOULDER!" From there, some of the parents in the stands picked up on the mantra and added their own voices to the chorus, ***"STOP DROPPING YOUR SHOULDER!"*** This became so frustrating to Julie because, try as she might, she just couldn't seem to stop dropping her shoulder. As a result, she would often either pop out or top the ball, squibbing a slow roller to the infield. No matter how hard she tried, she just couldn't seem to stop "dropping her shoulder."

It wasn't until I was playing baseball at Concordia College in Portland, OR that I realized why Julie couldn't overcome her little problem. One of my elective classes was entitled "Baseball Theory," which for the baseball enthusiast like myself was AWESOME! And, it was *much* more enjoyable than Humanities. In that class, one of the books we were required to read was *The Art of Hitting .300* by Charlie Lau.[1] The interesting thing about Lau was that he was never a .300 hitter himself (or even a starter for that matter) in his eleven years in the Majors. However, he would become an incredible hitting coach who Lou Piniella said was "the greatest batting instructor of them all."[2] After watching hours and hours of video tape of all the greatest hitters (Carew, Brett, Rose, Ruth, Aaron, Musial, DiMaggio, etc.), Charlie Lau was able to identify several common denominators that all the greats shared. And, in the process, he also dismantled two of the biggest lies that little league coaches across the country had been preaching for years.

One of those lies was that batters need to hit off their back foot.

Lau argued convincingly that not only did none of the greats hit off their back foot, but that it is, in fact, *impossible* to hit well while keeping your weight on your back foot. It's all just a matter of physics. If you don't transfer your weight from your back foot to your front foot, then you will generate very little kinetic energy into your swing and, therefore, into the ball. Also, it results in dropping your back shoulder, causing you to pop the ball up. Here's how Lau put it: "The ultimate cause of uppercutting is improper weight shift. If you tell a player…that you hit off your back foot, you seal his fate as an uppercutting hitter."[3] And just like that, I realized, Julie "dropping her shoulder" was not the problem but only a symptom. As long as Julie was just addressing the symptom and not the cause, she was fighting a losing battle. On the other hand, if she had had a coach who could have helped her to focus on proper weight transfer and hitting down on the ball slightly, the symptom of "dropping her shoulder" would have taken care of itself.

Pornography (or any sexual sin or any other addiction) is not the problem, my friend. It's just a symptom. And just as "STOP DROPPING YOUR SHOULDER!" was not going to free my sister from popping the ball up, "STOP LOOKING AT PORNOGRAPHY!" is not going to set you free. It didn't work for me, for Brian, for Jon, for Chase, and it will not work for you either. Again, *"Do not handle! Do not taste! Do not touch!...have an appearance of wisdom…but they lack any value in restraining sensual indulgence."*[4] These rules don't have *any value* because they don't have any power because they are just...*rules*...which only address the symptoms.

As you read the stories of myself, Brian, Jon, and Chase, no doubt you noticed a lot of similarities. For one thing, and as we just mentioned, white knuckling and battling could not set any of us free. On the contrary, each of us and all of us were set free by our faith in what Jesus had already done for us and/or our coming to realize and believe how God truly felt about us. Furthermore, God healing the deep wounds in our hearts enabled us to overcome our doubts. In other words, Jesus dug down deep to get to the root of the problem and there he touched the heart of the issue with his healing hands.

Walking in freedom is not a methodology where if you do this or that and you do it in a certain way, then you can be free. Remember what the Holy Spirit showed me: *I didn't have a pornography problem as much as I had a Gospel problem.* I believed that Christianity was hard. And it *was* hard because I was doing it with my own strength. I was *battling,* but I wasn't *believing.* ***I had a faith problem.*** Jesus had said I was free, but I didn't really believe him. It all comes back to faith.

In the process of writing this book, I sent the first fifteen chapters to Brian, Jon, and Chase so that they could get a feeling for what I was writing and to help give them direction as to what to share about their own journeys. After Jon had read what I had written, he asked if he could share it with someone he was trying to help in this area. Because I care more about people getting free than writing a book, I agreed to this even though I was still far from finished. Afterwards, Jon shared with me his friend's conclusions. Jon texted me that Tom (not his real name) read my book twice and really liked it *but* disagreed with me that living in freedom is *easy.* I texted back, "I didn't say it was easy. *Jesus did.*[5] I simply agreed with him." At this point, I abandoned the whole texting thing (which I don't love anyway) and called Jon directly and explained further, "Of course, several years ago, *I* didn't believe it was easy either. Tom's just not there in his journey yet."

Again, faith (or trust) is the hardest part about being a follower of Jesus. And it's difficult to believe we are free when we've just messed up. Right? Yet, that is what Jesus calls us to do. When asked, *"What must we do to do the works God requires?"*, Jesus responded, *"The work of God is this: to believe in the one he has sent."*[6] I assert Jesus wasn't just talking about believing he was the Messiah (although it included that) but also trusting him with your life and believing everything he said. Isn't that truly believing in someone? And ***he said,*** *"If the Son sets you free, you will be free indeed."*[7] Jesus isn't just your savior. He is also your deliverer, your healer, and the One who gives you his Holy Spirit.

So, what if you blow it then? What if you believe that Jesus set you free and you declare your freedom and have some success but then you fall off the wagon and succumb to temptation? That proves you're not free, right? I don't believe that. In fact, my trust in the Father's love for us, in Jesus's complete authority, and the Holy Spirit's empowering presence trumps any temporary setback or circumstance we might encounter. On the other hand, those setbacks do prove that we're human, that our faith still needs to grow, and that we have not arrived yet on our journeys. However, we're on the way, and our arrival is an absolute certainty.

One of my favorite stories about Jesus is where he calms a storm. After sharing some stories on the shores of the Lake of Galilee about what the kingdom of God is like, he says to his disciples, *"Let us go over to the other side."* So, everyone climbs in a boat, and off they go. Jesus, of course, is not a fisherman or a sailor but a carpenter, so he leaves the sailing to those proficient in the art while he takes a nap. And while Jesus is sawing some logs in the stern of the boat, a furious storm blows in and his disciples freak out. Waking him, they exclaim, *"Teacher, don't you care if we drown?"* Jesus calmly gets up and rebukes both the wind and the waves, telling them, *"Quiet! Be still!"* And the wind and waves obey him because he is their Author and Creator, so they are subject to him. Then, while the disciples are picking their jaws up off the deck of the ship, Jesus asks them, *"Why are you so afraid? Do you still have no faith?"* At this, the disciples are both dumbfounded and terrified as they realize that Jesus is no mere teacher.[8]

For those of us who recognize that we have not yet arrived, this story provides so much encouragement and hope. First of all, Jesus promised that we're going to the other side. This is why we can have as much peace as Jesus had while he snoozed in the middle of a raging storm. Second, he is in our boats *with us.* We are not traveling alone, and he will never leave us nor forsake us.[9] In fact, he literally indwells us, his followers, through the Spirit of God. And finally, there is no obstacle that he cannot overcome, because *he is God!* Jesus has authority over all! This is why demons submitted to him and did what he told them to do. Whether it's nature, the powers of Hell itself, pornography, lust, or any addiction for that matter, *Jesus is Lord of all!* This is why the Scripture declares emphatically, *"He who began a good work in you will carry it on to completion until the day of Christ Jesus."*[10] And this why your Father and your Lord can be so patient with you: **he knows that you realizing your freedom is a foregone conclusion.**

So, what do you do if you stumble? You do this: you get up, brush yourself off, and run to first base. *You believe!* Declare that Jesus has set you free and that you are free indeed. Declare that he loves you *perfectly*. Declare that he will never abandon you. Don't just think it. *Say it…out loud…and believe it. Believe him* and take him at his Word.

At the writing of this very sentence, it has now been almost seven years of walking in freedom. Of course, the temptations never really go away. Sometimes those temptations are stronger than at other times. I live in the same fallen world you do. Sometimes my eyes see things I wish they wouldn't, and the desire for forbidden fruit is aroused once again. Each time, I find myself at a crossroads – whether to linger or to choose freedom. I could very easily walk myself back into that cage of lies I lived in for thirty-seven years just because I lingered a moment longer than I should have before declaring my freedom. However, I know the truth now. And once you know the truth and *believe it*, those lies no longer have power over you.

Of course, you've got to want it too. You've got to want to be free. If you're not sure you do, then pray this prayer with me, "Lord, help me to want with all my heart what you want for me." And then pray this prayer again, and again, and again…and keep praying it until it is your reality. Again, *"for it is God who works in you to* ***will*** *and to act in order to fulfill his good purpose."*[11] You may not have arrived yet, but you are on the way, my friend, and Jesus is taking you to the other side. He is in your boat, and your freedom is a foregone conclusion. Believe it, live it, and keep steppin'!

Acknowledgments

As I look back over my life, I recognize that God was there all along leading me towards freedom. I am so grateful to the following friends and family members whom God used so instrumentally in my journey to freedom:

Thank you, Denise, my bride, my heart, my love, and my best friend. As I struggle with trying to find just the right words that convey how much you mean to me, I find my mind drifting back to our wedding day all those years ago when I sang to you about how, while I might not be sure where God would lead me, I was committed to following him, and was *absolutely sure* I wanted you with me on that journey. Thank you for taking this road with me. Through all the flats and breakdowns, you've loved me, believed in me, and encouraged me. Through you, *more than any other single person or thing,* God has taught me what grace and faithfulness truly look like. Without a doubt, you are the most profound part of my journey to freedom.

Thank you, Caleb, Austin, and Chase. You already know this, but I can't help myself but to put it in writing so all can see and know how much you, my sons, mean to me. Psalm 127 shows us that children are a reward from the Lord; they are *"like arrows in the hands of a warrior"* and *"blessed is the man whose quiver is full of them."* I, among men, am mostly richly blessed! I feel safe and secure because of you three, *my arrows*. I do not fear old age or frailty or being outnumbered or shamed by any man, for I know that *my arrows* are bold, ready, steady, and true. Each one of you is my favorite (don't tell the other two). And especially thank you, Chase, for the courage to share your journey to freedom within these pages.

Thank you, Brian and Iris Ellingson, for your tremendous friendship through these many years. It has been so rewarding and *so fun* to do life together with you guys this past decade. Thank you for partnering with us in the great experiment we call Gateway Church. Thank you, Brian, for walking shoulder to shoulder with me as we *both* realized our freedom in Christ simultaneously. Thank you for sharing your own story in this book and for the courage it took to do so. Thank you for caring more about helping people than your reputation. Denise and I are so excited to see how God is going to use you as a couple to make an eternal difference in the Tri-Cities and the world.

Thank you, Jon and Julie Carter. Julie, I am so blessed to have a sister like you. Your faithfulness to Jesus is awe-inspiring, and you make me want to press in and love him more. Jon, thank you for not giving up on yourself, Julie, your kids, and Jesus. As long as Jesus is in the mix, it's *never* hopeless. Thank you both for being willing to use your "regeneration" story to help others and for sharing it in this book. I love comeback stories. I love *your* story!

Thank you, Mom and Dad. Although Mom is no longer with us in body, I write these words trusting that she can see them from the other side. After all, I know that, because of Jesus, she's not a "was" but an "is." She *lives* and is with Christ. So, thank you, Mom, for always believing in me and for challenging me to "just do it" long before *Nike* made those words famous. Thank you, Dad, for also believing in me, for coaching my teams, and for telling me, *pretty much every day,* that you love me. We had our faults and tough times, but I absolutely loved my childhood and having you both as my parents.

Thank you, Jeff Plake, one of my very best friends ever, a true brother. Like you reminded me at the start, we always talked about doing something special together after we hung up our yo-yos. I hope this is just one of many special *somethings.* Thank you so much for contributing your tremendous gift with words and grammar to this endeavor as my editor. Not only did you do an incredible job, I had a lot of fun learning from you more about the English language as well as furthering my knowledge of logic.

Thank you, Emily Jimenez, who created the beautiful cover for this book. Thank you for making my vision come to life…and for letting me be picky.

Thank you, Michael Lee, for being my "wingman" for all these years. Thank you for believing me and all the times you challenged me to step out of my comfort zone.

Thank you, Gary and Paula Hays and thinkSMALL. Thank you for saying "yes" to God, having the courage to step into a new paradigm, and giving your lives for the Gospel so that kids all over the world might know Jesus and eternal life. And thank you, Gary, for writing the forward for this book.

Thank you to all the pastors, teachers, and special people who have invested in my life in such meaningful ways through all these years (some of which are no longer with us on this side of eternity): Daniel Westerfield, my very first pastor, who introduced me to Jesus, *"the friend who sticks closer than a brother"* (Proverbs 18:24); LaRene Westerfield-Cross, Julie Westerfield-Horn, Terri Westerfield-Myers, and my cousin Daryl Horn, who, when I was a brand new Christian and so rough around the edges, befriended me (as a result, I so looked forward to going to church *every* Sunday); Daniel Pecota, who taught me how to correctly handle the Word of Truth; Darrell Hobson, who taught me how to think; Dennis Leggett, whose true authenticity helped me drop my guard; Mel Ming, whose zest for life and love for all made me want to draw closer to

Jesus; Jim Ritchie, whose genuine concern for me as a person is why I am in the ministry today; Tom and Rita Davis, who took a chance on me, believed in me, and, *most importantly,* let me marry their daughter, Denise; Gene Arnold, whom God used to show me that pastoring was my niche; Daren Lindley, who taught me that "loving Jesus is the whole pie"; Dave Veach, who helped me pick up the pieces when our church plant failed and who challenged me to not be afraid of 'making a mess'; Dave Edler, for befriending me, mentoring me, and cheering me on as I began to put pen to paper; Wendy Walters, who, although we barely met through one of your workshops, God used profoundly to show me that *I could really do this* and to focus on the eternal opportunities that sharing my story could create; and the list goes on and on!

Thank you, Gateway Church. I love our church family and being your pastor. Thank you for trusting me when I felt God wanted us to try doing church at tables rather than in rows. Wow! What an incredible new frontier we have discovered together! And thank you for that incredible motivational push you gave me when I first announced that I was writing a book about my journey to freedom. Most of all, thank you for just accepting me all those times I mustered up the courage to be honest, transparent, and vulnerable with you about my struggles. Years ago, God gave me a vision (like as in a waking dream) of a church where I was the pastor and where the people were so accepting that it would bring tears to your eyes. I truly believe that Gateway is that church realized and in the flesh.

Most of all, thank you, Father, for being my *Abba* and for your perfect love for me. Thank you, Holy Spirit, for indwelling me and for never leaving me nor forsaking me no matter how much I messed things up. And thank you, Jesus, my savior, my healer, my redeemer, for being so patient with me, so good to me, dying for me, and setting me free. I love you with all that is within me and am so, so grateful to you.

NOTES

Chapter 1 – "FREEDOM!"

1. Hebrews 4:12
2. Job 31:1
3. John 10:27
4. Matthew 5:27-28

Chapter 2 – "You're Already Free!"

1. Wayne Cordiero, *The Divine Mentor* (Bloomington, MN: Bethany House, 2007), 102-105
2. Seth Taylor with David Glenn Taylor, *Feels Like Redemption* (Los Angeles, CA: Fireproof Ministries Inc., 2015, 2019)
3. Taylor, *Feels Like Redemption*, 46-47
4. Taylor, *Feels Like Redemption*, 43 [Emphasis mine]
5. Taylor, *Feels Like Redemption*, 43

Chapter 3 – First Things First

1. This quote is often attributed to Albert Einstein though the original author is unknown.
2. Author unknown
3. Matthew 3:1-2
4. Mark 1:14-15
5. Mark 6:12

6. Acts 2:37-38
7. Acts 26:20
8. Metanoia definition, *Merriam-Webster.com*. https://www.merriam-webster.com/dictionary/metanoia?utm_campaign=sd&utm_medium=serp&utm_source=jsonld
9. Guy Nave, *The Role and function of Repentance in Luke-Acts* (Atlanta, GA: Society of Biblical Literature, 2002). Also check out Mark J. Boda and Gordon T. Smith, eds., *Repentance in Christian Theology* (Wilmington, DE: Michael Glazier, 2006)
10. Edward J. Anton, *Repentance: A Cosmic Shift of Mind and Heart* (Spring Hill, TN: Discipleship Publications, 2005), 32-33
11. Romans 10:9-10
12. Mark 10:18
13. Romans 12:2
14. Hebrews 13:8
15. John 8:31-32, 36
16. John 8:36
17. Mark 1:15

Chapter 4 – Is Christianity Hard?

1. Revelation 21:4
2. Matthew 10:22, Mark 10:29-30, 2 Timothy 3:12, 1 Peter 4:12-14
3. Mark 12:30
4. Matthew 11:28-30
5. Luke 9:23

Chapter 5 – What Is "the Gospel?"

1. Mark 1:14-15
2. Millar Burrows, *The Origin of the Term "Gospel,"* from the *Journal of Biblical Literature* (Atlanta, GA: Society of Biblical Literature, 1925), Vol. 44, 21

Chapter 6 – Why the Gospel Is Easy

1. 2 Corinthians 6:14
2. 1 Timothy 6:15-16 [Emphasis mine]
3. Hebrews 12:29
4. Exodus 33:18
5. Exodus 33:19-20
6. 1 John 4:8
7. Ephesians 1:4-5
8. Romans 3:22-25
9. Hebrews 10:19-22
10. 1 Timothy 2:13

11. Colossians 1:27

Chapter 7 – The Half-Truth 'gospel' Many Believe

1. Hebrews 13:8
2. 1 John 4:8
3. J.D. Greear, *GOSPEL: Recovering the Power that made Christianity Revolutionary* (Nashville, TN: B&H Publishing Group, 2011), 44
4. John 8:32
5. Hebrews 13:5
6. Revelation 12:10-11
7. John 8:31-32 [Emphasis mine]
8. John 8:44
9. Luke 17:10
10. James 2:24
11. 1 Timothy 1:15
12. 1 Timothy 1:16
13. Romans 3:22-25
14. Ephesians 2:12
15. John 3:17
16. 1 Corinthians 14:33
17. Matthew 12:25
18. Matthew 11:30
19. John 8:36
20. Romans 3:4
21. John 17:17
22. John 8:36

Chapter 8 – Discovering Faith

1. 1 John 2:5-6 [Brackets mine]
2. 1 John 5:13
3. Thom S. Rainer & Eric Geiger, *Simple Church* (Nashville, TN: B&H Publishing Group, 2011), 14
4. 1 Corinthians 11:1
5. John 17:3 [Brackets and emphasis mine]
6. Ephesians 1:4-5
7. Ephesians 2:8-9
8. James 2:19
9. Hebrews 11:6
10. Hebrews 11:1 [Emphasis mine]
11. Hebrews 13:5
12. Luke 14:33
13. Philippians 2:13

14. Matthew 22:37-40
15. Bob Marley, *Three Little Birds* (Universal Music Corp. o/b/o Fifty-Six Hope Road Music Limited and Universal Music Corp. o/b/o Blackwell Fuller Music Publishing, 1977)
16. David Watson, *Called & Committed* (Wheaton, IL: Harold Shaw Publishers, 1982), 8
17. John 10:25-27
18. Hebrews 4:12
19. Hebrews 12:2
20. Colossians 1:3-6 [Emphasis mine]
21. John 13:35
22. 2 Corinthians 5:21
23. James 2:17
24. 1 John 3:18
25. James 1:22-25
26. Isaiah 61:1; Luke 4:16-21
27. John 14:23-24
28. J.D. Greear, *GOSPEL: Recovering the Power that Made Christianity Revolutionary* (Nashville, TN: B&H Publishing Group, 2011), 193
29. Ephesians 2:4
30. Bob George, *Classic Christianity* (Eugene, OR: Harvest House Publishers, 1989), 62-63
31. Hebrews 9:26
32. George, *Classic Christianity*, 52

Chapter 9 – My Epiphany

1. J. Avildsen (Director). (1984). *The Karate Kid* [Film]. Delpi II Productions
2. Job 31:1
3. Galatians 3:24
4. Colossians 2:20-23 [Emphasis mine]
5. J.D. Greear, *GOSPEL: Recovering the Power that made Christianity Revolutionary* (Nashville, TN: B&H Publishing Group, 2011), 21
6. Ephesians 3:4-5
7. Colossians 1:27
8. 1 Timothy 2:4
9. John 8:31-32
10. Matthew 9:22; Mark 5:34; Mark 10:52; Luke 8:48; Luke 18:42
11. Luke 17:9
12. Luke 7:50
13. Romans 1:17

Chapter 10 – ~~My~~ OUR First Win!

1. Genesis 3:6
2. Genesis 3:5 [Emphasis mine]
3. Genesis 3:4
4. Gregory Carroll and Doris Payne, *Just One Look* (Atlantic Recording Corporation, 1963)
5. Colossians 2:20-23
6. Abraham H. Maslow, *The Psychology of Science* (New York, NY: Harper and Row, 1966), 15

Chapter 11 – Divine Power

1. Philippians 3:2-3 [Emphasis mine]
2. 2 Corinthians 10:3-4
3. 1 John 1:5
4. Exodus 34:6, 1 Chronicles 16:34, Psalm 25:8
5. Ephesians 1:18-20
6. Matthew 17:20
7. Bob George, *Classic Christianity* (Eugene, OR: Harvest House Publishers, 1989), 171
8. John 4:46-53
9. James C. Collins, *Good to Great: Why Some Companies Make the Leap…and Others Don't* (New York, NY: HarperCollins), 1
10. 2 Corinthians 10:5
11. 2 Corinthians 10:4
12. Revelation 12:10
13. Revelation 12:11 [Brackets mine]
14. John 8:32

Chapter 12 – The Power of HIS Words

1. Ephesians 6:10-18
2. Ephesians 6:10 [Emphasis mine]
3. John 14:6
4. 1 Corinthians 1:30
5. Ephesians 2:14
6. Isaiah 9:6
7. Ephesians 6:17 [Emphasis mine]
8. Ephesians 6:18 [Emphasis mine]
9. Ephesians 6:17
10. Joseph Thayer, *Thayer's Greek Lexicon,* (Electronic Database by Biblesoft, Inc., 2002, 2003, 2006, 2011) as cited on *Blue Letter Bible* (2021), www.blueletterbible.org/lang/lexicon/lexicon.cfm?t=kjv&strongs=g4487
11. 2 Peter 1:20-21

12. Hebrews 4:12
13. Genesis 1:4
14. Genesis 1:6, 9, 11, 15, 24, 30
15. Mark 1:9-12 (NOTE: Some believe that Jesus being "in the wilderness" is symbolic language for Jesus being not just outside the city limits but that he was surrounded by the host of hell and that *"with the wild animals"* is symbolic language for demons. This makes sense to me as Satan and the forces of hell had a lot to gain by compromising the Son of God, and they had a lot to lose if God accomplished his plan through Jesus)
16. Luke 4:2
17. John 8:44
18. 1 Corinthians 15:45-49
19. Luke 4:3
20. Luke 4:4
21. Deuteronomy 8:3-4
22. Mt. 6:25-34
23. Luke 4:8 and Deuteronomy 6:13
24. Luke 4:10-11 and Psalm 91:10-11
25. Hebrews 10:1-18
26. Matthew 4:7 and Deuteronomy 6:16

Chapter 13 – The Power of Being in Jesus

1. John 1:1-5, 14, 18
2. John 1:1 [Emphasis mine]
3. Robert Zemeckis (Director). (1985). *Back to the Future* [Film]. Universal Pictures and Amblin Entertainment
4. Fausto Aarya De Santis, "Heraclitus – An Introduction to Flux and Logos," *Exposures of a Nomad*, October 24, 2010, www.faustoaarya.wordpress.com/2010/10/24/heraclitus-an-introduction-to-flux-and-logos/. Also, "Heraclitus and the Birth of Logos," *Modern Stoicism*, February 15, 2013, www.modernstoicism.com/heraclitus-and-the-birth-of-the-logos/, excerpts from Tom Butler-Bowdon, 50 *Philosophy Classics* (Hatchett, UK: Nicholas Brealey, 2013)
5. John 8:31-32 NASB
6. Ephesians 6:17
7. Lana Wachowski and Lilly Wachowski (Directors). (1999). *The Matrix* [Film]. Warner Bros., Village Roadshow Pictures, Groucho II Film Partnership, and Silver Pictures
8. John 8:36
9. 2 Corinthians 10:3-5

Chapter 14 – Sympathy or VICTORY?

1. Romans 7:14-15, 18-23Morgan Lee, "Here's How 770 Pastors Describe Their Struggle with Porn," *Christianity Today*, January 26, 2016, www.christianitytoday.com/news/2016/january/how-pastors-struggle-porn-phenomenon-josh-mcdowell-barna.html
2. David Kinnaman, "The Porn Phenomenon," *Barna*, February 5, 2016, www.barna.com/the-porn-phenomenon/#.VqZoN_krIdU
3. Ibid
4. Read John 5:1-9
5. John 5:5 NASB
6. John 5:6
7. In the footnotes of the NIV for John 5:4, it says this: "Some manuscripts include here, wholly or in part, *...and they waited for the moving of the waters.* [4] *From time to time an angel of the Lord would come down and stir up the waters. The first one into the pool after each such disturbance would be cured of whatever disease they had.*
8. John 5:7
9. Greg Koukle, "Never Read a Bible Verse," *Stand to Reason: Clear-Thinking Christianity*, February 4, 2013, www.str.org/w/never-read-a-bible-verse
10. Romans 6:6
11. Romans 6:14
12. Romans 6:17-18
13. Romans 6:22
14. Romans 6:14
15. Proverbs 18:24
16. Romans 6:15
17. Romans 7:1-4
18. Romans 8:4
19. Romans 7:7, 13
20. Romans 7:24-25
21. Romans 8:1-2 [Emphasis mine]
22. Romans 8:9-11
23. Matthew 9:16-17
24. Romans 8:37

Chapter 15 – "Show Me – Sand the Floor..."

1. Galatians 3:10 – *For all who rely on the works of the law are under a curse, as it is written: "Cursed is everyone who does not continue to do everything written in the Book of the Law."*
2. Galatians 3:11 – *Clearly no one who relies on the law is justified before God, because "the righteous will live by faith."*
3. John Eldridge, *Wild at Heart* (Nashville, TN: Thomas Nelson, Inc., 2001), 72

4. Titus 2:11-12
5. Hebrews 10:10
6. 2 Corinthians 5:17
7. E.g., Romans 1:7 – Paul addresses the church (in this case, the church in Rome) as "saints," which literally means "holy ones" or "holy people" (as the NIV translates it in this verse).
8. Philippians 1:6
9. 1 Peter 2:9 – *But "He are a chosen people, a royal priesthood, a holy nation, God's special possession, that you may declare the praises of him who called you out of darkness into his wonderful light.*
10. Hebrews 13:5
11. Philippians 4:13 (NOTE: the context of this verse is being content even in want; it does not mean that I can literally do "anything" like dunk a basketball over Lebron James)
12. 2 Peter 1:3-4 – *His divine power has given us everything we need for a godly life through our knowledge of him who called us by his own glory and goodness. Through these he has given us his very great and precious promises, so that through them you may participate in the divine nature, having escaped the corruption in the world caused by evil desires.*
13. Ephesians 2:10
14. 1 Peter 1:18-19 – *For you know that it was not with perishable things such as silver or gold that you were redeemed from the empty way of life handed down to you from your ancestors, but with the precious blood of Christ, a lamb without blemish or defect.*
15. John 8:36 and Galatians 4:7
16. John 8:36
17. Hebrews 4:12-13
18. J. Avildsen (Director). (1984). *The Karate Kid* [Film]. Delpi II Productions

Chapter 16 – Brian's Journey: "This is NOT *Jurassic Park*!"

1. Kutless, *Sea of Faces* (BEC Records, 2004)
2. Ted Roberts, *Pure Desire* (Bloomington, MN: Bethany House Publishers, 1999, 2008)
3. Seth Taylor with David Glenn Taylor, *Feels Like Redemption* (Los Angeles, CA: Fireproof Ministries Inc., 2015, 2019)
4. John 1:12-13

Chapter 17 – Jon's Journey: Life from Ashes

1. Dan Allender, *To Be Told* (Colorado Springs, CO: WaterBrook Press, 2005)
2. John 3:16
3. Luke 4:13
4. Stuart Hazeldine (Director). (2017). *The Shack* [Film]. Lionsgate Films

5. John Eldridge, *Wild at Heart* (Nashville, TN: Thomas Nelson, Inc., 2001), 72
6. Jay Stringer, *Unwanted* (Colorado Springs, CO: NavPress, 2018), xx
7. Philippians 2:13

Chapter 18 – Chase's Journey: "One Thing I Do Know"

1. J.R.R. Tolkien, *The Return of the King* (London, UK: George Allen & Unwin, 1955), 325
2. John 10:10
3. John Piper, Desiring God. (August 14, 2017). *You Are Not Addicted: The Power to Resist Pornography* [Video] YouTube. https://www.youtube.com/watch?v=9aAoHzts28Q&t=7s
4. John 8:36 and 2 Corinthians 5:7
5. Romans 6:4-7
6. Romans 6:14
7. Philippians 2:13
8. John 19:30
9. 2 Corinthians 5:21
10. John 9:25 [brackets and emphasis mine]

Chapter 19 – Keep Steppin'!

1. Charley Lau with Alfred Glossbrenner, *The Art of Hitting .300* (New York, NY: E.P. Hutton, Inc., 1980)
2. Lou Piniella with Bill Madden, *Lou: Fifty Years of Kicking Dirt, Playing Hard, and Winning Big in the Sweet Spot of Baseball* (New York, NY: HarperCollins, 2017), 329
3. Lau, *The Art of Hitting .300*, 114
4. Colossians 2:21-23
5. Matthew 11:28-30
6. John 6:29
7. John 8:36
8. Mark 4:35-41
9. Hebrews 13:5
10. Philippians 1:6
11. Philippians 2:13

Meet Mel

Mel Steinmeyer, together with his wife, Denise, pastor Gateway Church in Kennewick, WA, where each Sunday they gather around tables rather than in rows. All the way back to his days at Northwest University, Mel has never felt comfortable doing church *as usual*. When others would say, "Well, that's the way we do things," Mel would counter, "But why?"

As a young pastor, Mel was intrigued by James 5:16: *"...confess your sins to each other and pray for each other so that you might be healed..."* In other words, we could all be healed if only we had the guts to tell the truth about our struggles and failures. Yet, Mel, like most of us, never felt safe to do so. Then one day, God showed Mel that if he wanted James 5:16 to become a reality for himself and the church he pastored, he had to lead and go first. This is what Mel has made his life mission: to go first in being honest about his own journey so others might know Jesus, be healed, and be set free.

Before Gateway Church, Mel was a motivational speaker for over a dozen years in elementary and middle schools throughout the United States, as well as parts of Canada, England, and Australia. He also performed at the White House's annual Easter Egg Roll on four separate occasions. Through yoyos and comedy, Mel encouraged well over a million children to excel at school and in their character so they could make a difference in this world.

Mel and Denise have three grown sons – Caleb, Austin, and Chase. They also have three fur babies – a Boxer named Finn (a rescue), a Chiweenie named Lulu (another rescue), and a Corgi named Sam. Mel's hobbies include bass fishing, fly fishing, and kayaking…and especially *kayaking for bass.* Mel also enjoys reading fantasy and spy novels, watching whodunits with Denise, and immersing himself in role-paying games with Austin and their nerdy friends. He grew up playing sports: baseball, football, soccer, basketball, etc. However, baseball was his favorite sport, which he played into college. His favorite football team is the Seahawks, while his favorite baseball teams are the Mariners and the Reds.

If you would like to talk with Mel (and/or Denise), Brian Ellingson, or Chase Steinmeyer, or to have one of them share at your church or event, or if you would like to learn more about Gateway's experiment of doing church at tables, you can contact Mel at m.l.steinmeyer@gmail.com. Or, if you would like to talk with Jon or Julie Carter, please visit their website at regenerationlife.com.

www.ingramcontent.com/pod-product-compliance
Lightning Source LLC
LaVergne TN
LVHW041333080426
835512LV00006B/425

* 9 7 9 8 2 1 8 1 3 4 8 9 1 *